YOU CAN MAKE IT WITHOUT A COLLEGE DEGREE

Books by the Same Author

Anyone's Son
Jobs For Weekends
There's Always a Right Job for Every Woman
Money, Jobs, and Futures
Women In Action
World's Fairs

YOU CAN MAKE IT WITHOUT A COLLEGE DEGREE

ROBERTA ROESCH

Foreword by
John C. Crystal

Prentice-Hall, Inc.
Englewood Cliffs, New Jersey

Prentice-Hall International, Inc., *London*
Prentice-Hall of Australia, Pty. Ltd., *Sydney*
Prentice-Hall Canada, Inc., *Toronto*
Prentice-Hall of India Private Ltd., *New Delhi*
Prentice-Hall of Japan, Inc., *Tokyo*
Prentice-Hall of Southeast Asia Pte. Ltd., *Singapore*
Prentice-Hall Hispanoamericana, S.A., *Mexico*
Whitehall Books, Ltd., Wellington, *New Zealand*
Editora Prentice-Hall do Brasil Ltda., *Rio de Janeiro*

© 1986 *by*

Roberta Roesch

All rights reserved. No part of this
book may be reproduced in any form or
by any means, without permission in
writing from the publisher.

For Phil . . .
My husband and my friend

Library of Congress Cataloging-in-Publication Data

Roesch, Roberta.
  You can make it without a college degree.

  Bibliography: p. 195
  Includes index.
  1. Vocational guidance—United States.
2. Job hunting—United States.   3. High school
graduates—Employment—United States.   4. Degrees,
Academic—United States.   I. Title.
HF5382.5.U5R64   1986   650.1'4   85-19348

ISBN 0-13-976820-3

ISBN 0-13-976812-2 {PBK}

Printed in the United States of America

CONTENTS

Author's Note   vi
Foreword   ix

I   WHY YOU DON'T NEED A COLLEGE DEGREE   1

1   College Isn't for Everyone   3

2   How Good Are Your Chances Without a Degree?   17

3   How to Discover What You Want to Do—and What You Can Do   37

II   HUNDREDS OF JOBS FOR THE NON-COLLEGE GRADUATE   61

4   Job Opportunities in the Trades, the Arts, and the Office...   63

5   ...Service Jobs, the Government, Business, Health Care, and Sales   79

6   What the Armed Forces Can Offer You   97

III   HOW TO GET THE SKILLS YOU NEED AND MARKET THE SKILLS YOU HAVE   105

7   Dozens of New Alternatives to College Education   107

8   Marketing Strategies for Finding a Job   131

9   Résumé, Letter, and Interview Tips for the Non-College Graduate   145

IV   HOW TO MOVE UP ONCE YOU'VE MOVED IN   161

10   Moving Up and On   163

11   Parting Advice From Those Who Have Made It   177

Resource Directory   195

Index   222

AUTHOR'S NOTE

Four out of five Americans are convinced that the cost of going to college is climbing at such a rapid rate that college is likely to be out of reach for a great many individuals in the foreseeable future. Many people cannot afford it. Some say "It isn't for me." Others simply aren't ready for it at the time they graduate from high school.

The pages that follow are for all of those people who—for one reason or another—have decided against going to college for the four-year degree. This includes:

- high school students and graduates (and high school dropouts, too)
- the growing number of men and women who change their jobs and career fields during their working lives
- the great many people who stop working a while and, then, when they want to return, wonder what direction to take if they don't have a college degree.

In no way is this book saying that a college degree is not good to have, if that's what you want and need. Instead its aim is to point out alternatives to the four-year degree and show that there's a whole world of options that lead to satisfying jobs and careers, and give people what they want from life.

Each chapter tells a story about people of every age and type who are doing interesting and fulfilling work and living first-class life styles without that four-year degree. They're inspiring models to follow as they demonstrate so well that you don't have to go to college for education and success.

To gather a wide range of stories and views I interviewed men and women from everywhere in the country. I also talked to leaders in the career counseling field to obtain their viewpoints. To a person, everybody agreed that college isn't for everyone and that, through our own directed efforts we can create our own opportunities and progress from one thing to another. In most cases, the

Author's Note

people who told their stories granted permission to use their names. A few requested anonymity and that request has been honored.

I learned many things in my interviews, as the following pages detail. One thing that stood out, again and again, was the fact that many achievers with the best jobs today are still in their 20s and 30s. Somehow, when I started my research I mistakenly thought the people I'd meet would be later-day Horatio Algers who would show it was easier a generation ago to succeed without a college degree than it is today. Instead I found hundreds of people from *today's* generation who were also rising to the top of their fields without a four-year degree.

But whether my subjects were 20 or several decades older, they all had a great deal in common.

Above all, they had a *skill* to offer, and they knew that what the workplace wants are special, well-developed skills. They had also taken full advantage of alternatives-to-college training to prepare themselves for that skill. In a large number of cases, they had chosen to work for themselves rather than for an employer, so entrepreneurship was alive and well, not only in businesses and services but also in artistic pursuits.

Quite often people who were working for an employer rather than themselves had placed themselves in environments where they could learn from successful people and get training on the job. Sometimes, but not always, these people without the four-year degree had found their opportunities in smaller firms and companies instead of large corporations. They'd discovered, to their advantage, that smaller companies are not always tied in to the built-in premise that they only want to hire college graduates with a B or higher score. To back up these findings, research shows that over the last decade the action has shifted to smaller companies and most new jobs that have been created are in these smaller firms.

Over and over again I learned that self-education played a major part in getting non-degree people from where they started to where they are now. Happily, self-education is available to all of us in that greatest university in the world—public libraries throughout the country. As I interviewed, I was also struck by the number of non-degree people who, because of the expertise they'd acquired through experience and self-education, had gone on to teach and lecture at distinguished colleges and universities. Many were the recipients of honorary doctoral degrees.

As the foregoing indicates, a great many people have had a part in the writing of this book and, although it's impossible to mention each one, I owe a tremendous "Thank you" to all of the organizations that assisted me with information; to the career counselors and specialists who provided so much research; and to the analysts and economists at the Bureau of the Census and Bureau of Labor Statistics who were so helpful to me. Their names are listed throughout the text or in the Resource Directory.

Special thanks are also due to all of the men and women who so generously shared their experiences, viewpoints, feelings, and stories; to Michele Fedorchak for her hours and hours of faithful typing; and, always and forever, to my husband and my family.

To everyone who gave help and support, I am very grateful.

Roberta Roesch
Westwood, New Jersey

FOREWORD

The author of this book may well be damned for daring to challenge the accepted wisdom of our age: "You have to have a college degree to get a good job." Yet, Roberta Roesch has the wit and the courage to see and to state that this "just ain't so." She also has the intelligence and experience to be able to show people from all walks of life—young and old—how to turn this crucial, if unorthodox, insight to their lifelong advantage. She does this by outlining practical strategies for breaking through the "no college degree" barrier and achieving success in today's job market.

Now, I am no scorner of college professors, nor do I have the slightest bit of ill will towards higher education. On the contrary I am a strong supporter of lifelong learning and a fervent admirer of true scholars and great teachers.

What I do object to is what I perceive to be the widespread practice of trying to sell a product called "higher education" for the wrong reason, i.e., that you cannot get a good job without it. Of course you can! From my years of experience in life and career planning, I know. The barriers in our employment system *can* be overcome with relative ease through clear thinking and well-directed actions.

In this book, Roberta Roesch has chosen the path of common sense illuminated by reality. This book offers such common sense and reality to everyone entering the work force without a college degree. It is a valuable service, long overdue.

John C. Crystal
Chairman, John C. Crystal Center for Life/Work Planning*

*Mr. Crystal is also the founder of the Crystal System, which formed much of the basis for the book *What Color Is Your Parachute?* by Richard Nelson Bolles and coauthor with Bolles of *Where Do I Go From Here With My Life?*

I

WHY YOU DON'T NEED A COLLEGE DEGREE

chapter one

College Isn't for Everyone

So what if you don't have a college degree? And what if you don't plan to get one after you finish high school and face the next step in your life?

Or what if you find—in your 30s or 40s—that you need something new and, momentarily, feel held back because you don't have a piece of paper that spells out a four-year degree?

Take heart! You are in excellent company—some of the best, in fact—because of the people who have made the most of their lives without a diploma that tells the world they had four years of college. As an example:

- Mystery writer P. D. James ended her formal education at age 16 and then continued to educate herself by reading avidly.
- Fashion designer Ralph Lauren took a post-high school job as a department store salesman and signed up for college courses at night. He soon found college was not for him, so he dropped out to join the Army. Later he used his selling experience to launch his career in fashion.
- Lucille Ball was a washout in her first dramatic school. But after she finished high school—without taking time for college—she got her act together again and put all her efforts behind her goal of breaking into show business.
- Helen Gurley Brown, the magazine editor who turned the failing *Cosmopolitan* magazine into a moneymaking success, left college after one semester because of financial reasons. Her alternative was business school and honing the skills that took her through seventeen office jobs before she got the copywriting job that led to her major breakthrough.
- Composer-singer Rod McKuen worked at all kinds of jobs—ranch hand, lumberjack, shoe salesman, cookie puncher—before he ultimately found his way to becoming the person he is today.
- Elizabeth Arden, the high priestess of cosmetics,

briefly pursued nurses' training prior to abandoning that choice and entering the cosmetics field via the first-job-in-an-office route.
* Stand-up comic Steve Martin studied philosophy at a state college and maintained a straight A average. But he became disillusioned and left to enroll in a television writing course.

Other notables without a degree have included such people as cartoonist, producer, and businessman Walt Disney; ex-President Harry Truman; the famous airline magnate Eddie Rickenbacker; Metropolitan Opera baritone Robert Merrill; Mary Kay Ash, founder of Mary Kay Cosmetics; Jack La Lanne of La Lanne Enterprises; actor Richard Thomas, John-Boy of television's "The Waltons;" and many other celebrated people.

There are also people you don't always know who succeed without a degree. There is Ed Zaborer, a highly successful restaurateur who got his start as an entrepreneur through selling hot dogs on a boardwalk. Today his spacious restaurant boasts one of the world's most valuable collections of Tiffany lamps, and his food and decor are so outstanding patrons line up for two or more blocks. There is Terry Dorman, who never made it to college. With a friend he began a screen-printing business that started with posters and T-shirts and later progressed to jobs for an industrial design firm. Subsequently an electronics company asked the partners to make displays for computers and other high-tech equipment. As this was such a big break, Dorman raised sufficient capital from his family to get into the electronic components field. In 1979 Dorman's partner sold out. However, by 1983, Dorman—while still in his 20s—was running a company that was grossing $7 million.

Another example is Cynthia Archer. After a two-year liberal arts secretarial course, she obtained a job as secretary to David Hartman of "Good Morning America." A typical day for Cynthia meant handling several sacks of mail, screening all of the phone calls, and speaking on the telephone to such celebrated individuals as Gerald Ford and Henry Kissinger. There is also G. Dale Murray who graduated from high school and enlisted in the Army with ten dollars in his pocket. After his discharge, he worked in construction for a year before entering the banking industry and developing special skills in mergers and acquisitions. Murray tried several college courses. However, he dropped out of each because he was eager to move on in the business world. After seven years in banking, he had acquired a more substantial portfolio than the president of his bank, so he went into business as a financial consultant. Today he is president of Murray Industries, a Delaware holding company, and when he went back to the twenty-fifth reunion of his high school class the man who left high school with ten dollars had an estimated worth of one hundred million dollars.

For an example of another color, Sherri Austin, a recognized authority in color analysis, went to college just long enough to know it wasn't for her. "After I finished high school and was headed for college to please my parents, I got a summer job in retailing and by the end of the summer was made assistant manager of the baby department," she said. "At that point the store offered me a chance to enter its buyer training program, and I begged my parents to let me do that instead of going to college. But they told me I should go to college and this was probably the worst mistake they ever made."

Sherri soon left the campus for a job in a packing corporation and stayed on to work as a secretary. Later she held such a variety of jobs that her grandmother told her, "A rolling stone gathers no moss."

"Many of the jobs were in marketing," she pointed out. "But I still kept changing periodically, always knowing that someday I would start my own business. For me, college would have been a waste because it could never have given me the experience I had with all of my jobs."

Admittedly there are some careers where a four-year degree is a "must" and there is no doubt college is a good choice when it is right for you. It is obvious, for example, that you will never be the world's top physicist without a string of degrees, and you cannot be "Lawyer of the Year" when the bottom line of your education is your high school diploma.

It is true that in some situations you will be able to go just so far without a college degree. However, you will see throughout this book how people have overcome this by educating themselves through other alternatives and rejecting the ingrained belief that we can only do those things for which we have a bachelor's degree saying that we have been trained to do them. So even though many jobs on the market require a four-year degree, there *is* a life after high school for people who don't go to college—and with the right decision and planning there are many opportunities and options that lead to satisfying and rewarding jobs and give you what you want out of life.

MYTHS ABOUT COLLEGE AND VIEWS FROM THE SPECIALISTS

Some of the crumbling myths include:

- You cannot make it in our society without four years of college.
- All the big money is wrapped up in a college degree.
- Vocational education is a "second choice."
- There is no place in America for people who work with their hands.

In their book *Getting Skilled*, Tom Hebert and John Coyne write: "Since our first book *This Way Out: A Guide to Alternatives to Higher Education* we have been wrestling with the common assumption that you need college to get ahead. The issue is still unresolved. There is no dramatic proof that simply going to college improves your lot in life. There can be no policy about this. It remains, even to the experts, an open question for the individuals."

A person who takes a stronger view of the guaranteed promise of college is Richard K. Irish, who, as author of the bestseller *Go Hire Yourself an Employer,* has more than 20 years of experience as a job counselor and executive search specialist. "College degrees and, above all, advanced degrees are among the biggest swindles in our society," he declares. "In my judgment, as many as two-fifths of those attending schools of higher education would be better financially and emotionally if they found work as sheet metal technicians, carpenter craftsmen, laboratory technicians and so forth where pay, security, and job satisfaction are *superior* to most jobs requiring a college degree."

John C. Crystal, regarded as one of the most influential career consultants in the United States, co-author with Richard Bolles of *Where Do I Go From Here With My Life?* and founder and chairman of the John C. Crystal Center for Creative Life/Work Planning, has this to say: "I resent the absolutely automatic assumption that college is a necessity for everyone. People should have an option to decide whether or not college is for them. If the education and training is going to be useful in their field, fine. But to go to college because everybody is going makes little sense."

Howard L. Shenson, formerly a professor of business administration at the University of Southern California and California State University and currently a specialist in the consulting industry, concurs. "As someone who has taught at universities, I value education," he maintains. "But the university has never been a substitute for practical experience. If you have a skill, talent, or ability to market to others, there are many situations in which a college degree is certainly not required and for some people it's more appropriate to get training in a practical skill."

Ronald C. Pilenzo, President of the American Society for Personnel Administration, who has had more than 20 years of experience in all facets of human resource management, agrees we are overdoing the feeling that everyone should go to college. "We've gone completely mad insisting that everyone should have a college degree," he says, "and in making it too accessible we dilute the value of the degree. I know many stories where parents tend to think their children should have something better than they had and so, in the belief that college will do magical things, they put their kids through college to study things that sometimes tend to be impractical when graduates go to look for a job. Counselors should point out alternatives."

GOOD REASONS TO CONSIDER ALTERNATIVES

According to Russell W. Rumberger, Senior Research Associate with the Institute for Research on Educational Finance and Governance at Stanford University, the job market for college graduates does not look that favorable during the next ten years, given the kind of jobs the economy will be producing.

In a research study on the market for college graduates from 1960 to 1990 published in the *Journal of Higher Education* in August 1984, he stated that between one-quarter and one-third of recent graduates report they are underemployed. "Moreover the problem is likely to become even more widespread in the decades ahead," he continues. "Most people believe that the economic benefits of education have no bounds. Yet considerable evidence suggests that the American workforce has already attained an educational level that exceeds the educational requirements of many jobs in the economy."

In many people's views, the current job prognosis is giving constant warning signals that many overeducated corporate types will be in great excess by the 1990s. One 32-year-old graduate who has had to buck this already did his undergraduate work at an Ivy League university and obtained his Ph.D. at a prestigious Graduate School of Applied and Professional Psychology. When it was time to job hunt he sent out 100 resumes for a corporate psychologist's job. Nearly 80 percent of the companies responded with nothing but a form letter.

Legions of other graduates are experiencing this dilemma and joining the ranks of the unemployed or, often, the underemployed. As one unemployed young graduate who studied philosophy and spoke both Japanese and French reported in *The New York Times:* "We're in a technical era, and skills are very necessary. Nietzsche and Plato are very successful in cocktail parties but not in the job market." In another case a graduate of a top university who could offer high grades and excellent credentials was unable to land even an entry level job in the field of his choice. Instead he held a series of jobs as a shoe salesman, painter, and clerk-typist. Another young woman who graduated cum laude from an eastern university began her job search for an entry level spot as a bilingual researcher or translator long before graduation day. However, when no job was forthcoming, she had to put her degree aside and continue working in the credit department of a store where she had worked part time while in college.

Unfortunately, this employment problem seems likely to continue because, like Russell Rumberger, Jon Sargent, an economist in the Division of Occupational Outlook, Bureau of Labor Statistics, emphasizes that the latest projections covering the 1982–95 period show that the keen competition for employment is not expected to abate appreciably. Says Sargent: "The job market for college graduates deteriorated beginning about 1970 with the rapid growth of the college-age population. People born during the post-World War II baby boom reached their late teens and early twenties and the flow of new college graduates into the labor force became a flood. Over the 5 years from 1969 to 1974, the number of bachelor's degrees awarded annually by the nation's colleges and universities increased by more than 200,000—from 729,000 to 946,000—and remained at a high level thereafter. Over the 1970–82 period, college graduates in the labor force doubled to 21 million."

As a result of this trend, the occupational pattern of college graduate employment changed greatly between 1970 and 1982, and the most striking change was the aforementioned increase in the proportion of college graduates employed in occupations that have not traditionally required a college education. In all, underemployed college graduates totaled more than 4 million in 1982—the accumulation of more than a decade of graduates who were unable or chose not to enter a job that required their level of education.

"Nearly 21 million college graduates are projected to enter the labor force between 1982 and 1995, an average of about 1,600,000 a year," continued Sargent. "As during the 1970s those graduates are expected to exceed the openings by as much as 4 million or 300,000 annually. In addition, the job market will be more competitive to the extent that currently underemployed graduates will vie with future entrants for college level jobs."

Along with being unemployed or underemployed, the frequency with which graduates used the course content of majors they spent four years studying varied by the field. In reporting on a survey conducted by the National Center for Education Statistics, Daniel E. Hecker and Douglas Braddock, labor economists in the Division of Occupational Outlook, Bureau of Labor Statistics, stated that the frequency with which graduates used the course content of their majors varied by field. Some graduates, especially those with social science or liberal arts majors, said they rarely or never used the course content of their majors in their jobs. Sixty-eight percent of history majors and sixty-three percent of political science majors gave this same response.

COLLEGE COSTS:
A $20,000 TO $60,000 NIGHTMARE!

The soaring costs of college are making four years of tuition and board a constantly growing nightmare for middle- and low-income people. Right now students attending, or planning to attend, four-year colleges and universities are facing the largest annual increase in education expenses ever reported, as fees are rising approximately 8 percent annually. At press time the American Council on

Education reveals that the cost of tuition, room and board at a typical public college is $4918, or more, per year. For a typical private college it is $9574 and up. Total costs at the most prestigious colleges top the $12,000 mark and at some private and Ivy League schools the cost is almost $15,000 per year—or a $60,000 investment for four years.

In a comprehensive public opinion study conducted in 1984 by Group Attitudes Corporation of New York City, a survey found that four out of every five Americans are convinced college costs are climbing at such a rate that college will be out of the reach of the average person in the foreseeable future. Three out of every four said they will be able to afford college costs only with the help of low-interest loans or grants.

At the same time college costs are rising, the value of financial aid available for college students is declining, according to the College Board in New York. In fact, allowing for inflation, the real value of student aid has dropped 21 percent in the 1980s. A study prepared by the Board's Washington office and funded by the Ford Foundation traced most of the drop to (1) the 1981 decision by the Reagan Administration and Congress to restrict eligibility for Guaranteed Student Loans and to phase out Social Security benefits for college students; and (2) to a drop in the use of veterans' benefits.

NOW—THE GOOD NEWS

While the supply of four-year-college graduates is exceeding the demand for jobs that require four years of college, thousands of people who received their training in two years or less at community and junior colleges; reputable vocational, technical, and business schools; apprenticeships; and company-sponsored programs are finding, and advancing in, jobs in business, industry, technology, paraprofessional areas, creative arts and crafts, and trades and services.

Often the people with this training are preferred for many openings. In fact, Don DeCamp, a vice-president at

Snelling & Snelling, which has 500 placement offices in the United States, reported in *The New York Times* that the number of college graduates who come for help in finding a job has increased tremendously since 1980. He also said that in job fields such as data processing, where there are often entry-level job openings, those who obtained specialized training at two-year schools are being hired much more quickly than the average college graduate.

In California, Sharon David-Shubin obtained her post-high school training at The Fashion Institute of Design and Merchandising. Since her graduation with an associate of arts degree, she has worked as a coordinator, a stylist, a sketch artist, and a full-fledged costume designer. She has been responsible for the costumes worn by performers during the half-time acts for Superbowls and has created the costumes for two Radio City Music Hall productions. She has also worked for Walt Disney Productions researching more than one hundred ethnic costumes displayed at Epcot World Showcase.

Across the country at New York Community College, Rocky Aoki, founder of the Benihana Enterprises chain of 50 Japanese restaurants, studied hotel-restaurant management. After graduation and a two-year degree, he saw an advertisement for rentals for ice cream trucks and immediately arranged to lease a truck. Mid-town New Yorkers didn't buy his product, so Aoki moved the truck to Harlem and earned enough money in four months to open a small Japanese restaurant called Benihana. Since the opening of that first successful restaurant more than 20 years ago, he has parlayed his success into a restaurant chain and several other pursuits.

As things stand now, the Bureau of Labor predicts that through the mid-1990s employment is expected to increase in almost all occupations. See Chapters four and five for the total picture of where the jobs will be.

For a capsule picture, the Bureau of Labor Statistics lists twenty occupations as those with the largest expected growth and, as you can see in Figure 1-1, many of the jobs do not require a four-year degree. (A longer list would show

FIGURE 1-1
TWENTY FASTEST GROWING OCCUPATIONS, 1982–95

Occupation	Percent growth in employment
Computer service technicians	96.8
Legal assistants	94.3
Computer systems analysts	85.3
Computer programmers	76.9
Computer operators	75.8
Office machine repairers	71.7
Physical therapy assistants	67.8
Electrical engineers	65.3
Civil engineering technicians	63.9
Peripheral EDP equipment operators	63.5
Insurance clerks, medical	62.2
Electrical and electronic technicians	60.7
Occupational therapists	59.8
Surveyor helpers	58.6
Credit clerks, banking and insurance	54.1
Physical therapists	53.6
Employment interviewers	52.5
Mechanical engineers	52.1
Mechanical engineering technicians	51.6
Compression and injection mold machine operators, plastics	50.3

NOTE: Includes only detailed occupations with 1982 employment of 25,000 or more. Data for 1995 are based on moderate-trend projections.

more occupations from the medical, financial, and business service industries.)

Add to the foregoing sampling of options the self-employment opportunities people create for themselves.

One example of the latter is tall, bearded Jean Deer. He began his job life in an auto body shop. "But by the time I was twenty-six, I was tired of fenders and doors, so I made the decision that somewhere there had to be a better way to make a living," he said. "A friend who was knowledgeable about photography suggested I look into that. As a first step

I bought a camera. But when I found I couldn't work it to get the results I wanted, I enrolled in photography school at night and worked in the body shop during the day."

Ultimately Deer made a specialty of outdoor portraiture with imagination and indoor photography with naturalness. Today he is respected professionally by top people in his field. Like others, he learned opportunities abound without a college degree when you find out what you want to do; head for the specialized training you need; inject yourself with the necessary drive; and go the extra mile in developing your own special talent or skill.

chapter two

How Good Are Your Chances Without a Degree?

Michele Hogan Schmidt is a dynamo who holds an exciting high-pressure job as public relations director for the Sheraton New Orleans Hotel. Michele—without a college degree—has advanced to a job many graduates would give their all to have.

"The main reason I didn't go to college was because a family situation made me realize in my senior year in high school that I must work to help support my sister and me," she explained. "In high school I was a member of the Cooperative Office Education program, and during the summer of my senior year I was placed in the Finance Division of the Department of Purchasing at City Hall in New Orleans. Since I was anxious to get experience, I worked in that office during Thanksgiving and Christmas vacations, too."

As soon as Michele got her high school diploma, she took a full-time civil service job as Typist-Clerk 1. However, she reached Steno 3 when she was 20 and discovered that there was no other place for her to go in the Purchasing Department. She transferred to a city department that governed all the architectural and structural changes.

"As I worked I learned by keeping my eyes and ears open," she said. "I knew I didn't have the college degree that many places required. But I felt from my observations that many of us without degrees can do many jobs as well if not better than many people with degrees in specialized fields."

With this as her credo Michele left the city's employment to work in the corporate world. Eventually she signed up with a temporary employment service. "My first job was in the public relations department of a major firm," she reported, "and when the temporary assignment was over I was asked to stay on as executive assistant to the public relations department. I remained till the public relations department was closed."

By then Michele had discovered she liked communications, so she did some free-lance public relations and worked for a magazine concerned with Louisiana life.

"After that I bluffed my way into an advertising agency," she confessed, "and stayed till I went to work for a woman who ran her own organization and had the Sheraton Hotel account."

Following that job, Michele took another public relations position. Subsequently, the New Orleans Sheraton called her and told her they would like to interview her for a job as director of their in-house public relations. "Again, I saw opportunity—and here I am," she smiled.

Terry Loebel, another high school graduate without a college degree, started with a post-high school job on an assembly line and is now a self-made millionaire, and founder and head of a direct mail distributing firm that produces and mails two billion coupons and offers per year. When he was laid off from his auto assembly line job, Loebel was so bored with his nonworking life that he read everything he could get his hands on, including the national brand coupons he received.

As a result, he came up with an idea to give local businesses the same opportunity as national brands to promote products and services through coupon mail offers. "I figured if it was good for Kellogg's it should also work for the drug store or dry cleaners," contended Loebel.

To get started, he borrowed $1,250 and began marketing the business under the name Val-Pak—short for valuable package. "The name just came to me," he recalled. "But I had never sold anything and I was scared out of my mind."

Going from business to business, Loebel convinced fourteen retailers to participate. After he designed their coupons, using a rented typewriter and graphics clipped from newspapers, Loebel had a local print shop reproduce the promotional offers. Twenty thousand homes were included in the initial mailing. The concept proved an immediate success, and several advertisers asked Loebel to expand the service to other cities. Today his sales network covers the country, and the company distributes promotional offers for local, regional, and national products and services to nearly one hundred million homes annually.

As for Loebel, he is proving, like many others that your chances *can* be good without a college degree. In fact, some people even say that they might not have made it if they had gone to college.

In her book *The Case Against College*, Caroline Bird points out the example of E. J. Cossman, who told Matt Dana for a chapter in *Instant Millionaires*, "If I had a college education, I would have gone to work for some big corporation, and I'd still be there." Instead Cossman blew the $276 he had when he got out of the armed forces to start a mail order export business that made him a $1,000,000. "If you're a real winner," writes Bird, "you don't have time for the professors and you don't care what the wise men say. You're too busy going for broke."

A former college professor agrees with this suggestion. "I taught from 1949 to 1977," he stated, "and left largely because I feel universities do a poor job of preparing students for life. Curriculums are dominated by what teachers want to teach. The faculty considers the marketability of its product totally irrelevant. I tried to change the system but grew discouraged and left."

"Don't tell me about a college degree," a disappointed parent asserted. "I gave my daughter what I thought was the best advantage. But now she doesn't know what she wants to do so she sits at home and does nothing. Four years of gainful employment would have shown her what she'd like to do and given her marketable skills."

In *The Complete Guide to Writing Nonfiction*, compiled by the American Society of Journalists and Authors (Writer's Digest Books, 1983), environmentalist Michael Frome writes: "Over the years I've been challenged because I lack a technical background in forestry and wildlife management; yet professional training in a given field is not a requirement for critical, objective useful examination. Think for a moment of some of those who came through experience and experiment. Mark Twain had a fourth- or fifth-grade education. John Muir, champion of nature and preservation, left the University of Wisconsin for what he calls the University of Wilderness. A university degree is like a license for employment, rather than a testament of knowledge and skills gained."

"Certainly a college degree is a requisite to open many doors but that doesn't mean doors can't be opened without it," Frome continued in an interview. "Come to think of it, Robert Frost didn't have a degree either, but he was in demand as a teacher, and he conducted workshops at hundreds of colleges."

THE CASE FOR COLLEGE WHEN YOU WANT AND NEED IT

Despite the foregoing viewpoints it is only realistic to bow to arguments for college for people who want and need it. To begin with, many people say college graduates fare better, on the average, than nongraduates, because the additional education is often an advantage in competing with nongraduates. In addition, the argument is often raised that, from a noneconomic point of view, the four years that lead to a college degree provide made-to-order opportunities for broadening interests; developing as a person, and establishing credibility. Over and above this, everyone knows that there are professional, managerial, and technical jobs you cannot hope to get without a degree.

"In the corporate world, the college degree can be the union card that gets you your entry," declared professional photographer Arthur Leipzig who—without a college degree—is also a full professor at C. W. Post College. "Still and all, if the quality of your work is good—and if you have drive—you will ultimately overcome not having the four-year degree, though you'll have to struggle more and it will take you longer. The real value of college is that it will speed up the process and give you that union card, so you're not locked out of choices."

"I have no idea what college would have done for me," comments Jean Deer. "All I know is that not having been there I don't miss it. I'm sure it gives you a background to call on. But day-to-day experiences do that, too."

"As a black female, the odds against success are awesome to begin with," maintains Sharon Morgan, vice president for public relations at Burrell Advertising, Inc. "Without college the odds are even greater. But it is possible. I started working as a cashier in a grocery store when I was in 8th grade. In high school I worked part time as a typist in a bank."

After high school, Sharon used the skills she had acquired at the bank in a job as an executive assistant in a hospital. She also took college courses and continued to develop the writing skills she had been refining since childhood. She soon gained a reputation for being able to do a variety of things.

"A few months after I got my job the hospital cut back on its staff and eliminated its public relations department," Sharon said. "I was kept on, however, because I could do many things. I'd learned about grants and fund-raising, for instance, so I became valuable for that."

Because of her value, the hospital soon offered Sharon a promotion and any job title she would like—as long as she continued writing grants. "I asked for 'Director of Community Services,'" she remembered, "because in that spot I could write grants, and also do public relations. Later, when a new hospital was being built, I suggested setting up a Community Development Corporation so I was appointed associate director of that."

In the meantime, Sharon discovered that college was not for her, so she got her alternative education through workshops, seminars, reading, and talking to people who did work she was interested in. She subsequently left the hospital for a job with a management consulting firm, as she felt management consulting would give her a different experience. After a year of that, she founded—at age 30—Morgan Communications Group, Inc., where she managed a five-person staff and served such accounts as Coca-Cola and Kentucky Fried Chicken.

When she had run this firm for three years and built a

business known as one of the most reputable black-owned firms in the industry, Sharon decided it was time to move on. The next step was approaching Burrell Advertising with the idea of creating a public relations department. When she convinced the company, she found herself with an entrepreneurial niche within a corporation. In this new trend in business called "intrapreneurship," intracompany entrepreneurs work within a company, and the company provides seed money, backing, and security.

"People have always been surprised when they found I didn't have a degree," Sharon commented. "But for every move I've made I've let my experience speak for me."

OTHER CORPORATE VIEWS

"Most of the people we hire in the management and business end of our company tend to fall into the college-educated category," stated Peter Acly, Assistant Manager of Corporate Issues for General Foods International. "Our secretarial pool and production people are also highly skilled, and even though, for some of these situations, people do not need the traditional education from a four-year college, they do need specialized training and expertise."

"The bottom line is that no set of rules is constant," he acknowledged. "But you have to have skills. You can't jump out of high school and get a job that's going to get you anywhere."

Gary A. Mainor, Director of Human Resources for the WCB Group Publishers, also points out that many professional jobs will be closed to people without a degree. "But there are other types of jobs that they can succeed in," he declares. "Since some firms don't place as high a premium on a college education, people without a degree should (1) search for these opportunities and sell their skills, (2) aim for positions they can realistically attain, and (3) be prepared to accept entry level jobs and work their way up through the organization. Many supervisors are not college graduates but gain their positions based on experience."

Ronald C. Pilenzo concurs that often the only way to overcome the lack of a degree is to have experience. "Unfortunately, applying at a place of business without a degree tends to move people to be considered for jobs that have less value and pay less," he said. "Right now this is a way of life in this country, and I think the problem is further complicated as people tend to hire in their self-image.

"But I have done work in large organizations where I have shown that a degree is not required, and in the process made the jobs more viable. Sometimes people are at a disadvantage without a degree only because others overvalue the need for it on a given set of jobs."

BUT STILL AND ALL...

Certainly the above is worth considering when you are deciding whether or not you are interested in a job or career that does not need the four-year degree. While you are weighing the pros and cons, it is wise to keep remembering that the number of jobs for which college is usually a prerequisite is rising more slowly than the number of graduates available for the jobs. Consequently, there is no way you can be really sure that a four-year college degree will enhance your chance for success. As Jon Sargent, the Bureau of Labor Statistics economist, re-emphasizes, "A college degree is not the reliable ticket to a good job that it once was."

John R. Coleman, a former president of Haverford College and now president of the Edna McConnell Clark Foundation, added in *Mainliner* magazine: "For a long time both colleges and employers have helped foster the idea that a degree was the key to status, income, and security. Never mind that the actual requirements of the job often bore little relation to what went into the preparation for the degree; what mattered was that the degree was a simple and automatic screening device for those employers who had more job-seekers than jobs. And never mind that the expectations created in this way often proved unrealistic.

"As many young college graduates can testify, neither status, income nor security is assured any longer by a degree. The piece of paper is often a door opener, but it is often not much more than that."

DOLLARS AND CENTS

We've all heard that during a lifetime the college graduate usually earns more money than the person with a high school diploma. It is true that in some cases the starting pay may be higher for college graduates who find work. But this is not *always* the case.

According to the latest available estimates by the Bureau of the Census, the *average* male college graduate who was 25 years old in 1979 will earn $1,165,000 from that year through age 64. A 25-year-old man with a high school education will earn about $861,100 from 1979 through age 64. Women will earn much less. In 1979 a 25-year-old female college graduate who worked full time all year round could expect to earn $772,000 in the rest of her lifetime—$557,000 less than her male counterpart.

These estimates, however, are the amounts that specific groups of people can expect to earn from 1979 through age 64. But a group is not an individual, and an individual's earnings depend on many factors that were not analyzed when the Census made the estimates. Among the important influences that were not used in the Bureau's analysis were (1) location of residence; (2) the kind of educational program pursued; (3) continuity of work experience; (4) occupation; and (5) motivation.

According to Peter Ward, a labor economist at the Bureau of Labor Statistics, the answer on earnings for many people is in Figure 2-1, which appeared in the Government's Occupational Outlook Quarterly, Fall 1983. The list ranks occupations by median weekly earnings for 1982 (the latest figures available at this writing). The median is

FIGURE 2-1

Earnings

Earnings in Jobs That Don't Require a College Degree

Rank and Occupation		1982 Median Weekly Earnings	1982 Employment (thousands)
1	Sales managers, except retail trade	$566	372
2	Structural metal crafts workers	497	81
3	Officials of lodges and unions	479	126
4	Officials and administrators, public	463	430
5	Other managers and administrators	463	6518
6	Millwrights	458	89
7	Telephone installers and repairers	449	304
8	Electric power line installers	441	110
9	Drillers, earth	441	53
10	Tool and die makers	437	156
11	Ticket station and express agents	434	154
12	Electricians	432	601
13	Railroad, car shop repairers	432	45
14	Mine operatives, nec.	432	222
15	Aircraft mechanics	431	130

Earnings in Jobs That Don't Require a College Degree—Continued

Rank and Occupation		1982 Median Weekly Earnings	1982 Employment (thousands)
38	Office machine repairers	373	78
39	Machinists	371	508
40	Cement and concrete finishers	370	55
41	Furnace tenders, stokers, except metal	369	67
42	Heavy equipment mechanics, including diesel	$366	946
43	Registered nurses	365	1415
44	Drafters	365	304
45	Lathe and milling machine operatives	362	83
46	Other mechanics and repairers	361	267
47	Air-conditioning, heating, and refrigeration mechanics	360	217
48	Job and die setters, metal	358	74
49	Dry wall installers, lathers	355	87
50	Excavating, grading machine operators	351	304
51	Other precision machine operatives	349	49

16	Data processing machine mechanics	429	84	52	Photographers	348	96
17	Blue-collar worker supervisors	422	1688	53	Furnace tenders, smelters, etc.	348	51
18	Plumbers and pipefitters	422	471	54	Sales workers, service and construction	346	268
19	Authors	421	69	55	Clerical supervisors, nec.	345	270
20	Purchasing agents and buyers, nec.	421	260	56	Printing press operators	345	182
21	Inspectors, except construction, public	420	107	57	Welders and flamecutters	345	602
22	Mail carriers, postal service	420	264	58	Painters and sculptors	344	208
23	Postal clerks	420	271	59	Advertising agents and sales workers	344	130
24	Crane, derrick, and hoist operators	420	120	60	Glaziers	344	50
25	Musicians and composers	410	149	61	Expeditors and production controllers	342	257
26	Sales representatives, wholesale trade	409	1020	62	Carpenters	341	1073
27	Inspectors, other	408	136	63	Meatcutters and butchers, except manufacturing	341	183
28	Police and detectives	405	505	64	Household appliance mechanics	340	150
29	Sheet metal workers, tinsmiths	401	140	65	Real estate agents and brokers	339	534
30	Electrical, electronic technicians	400	314	66	Radio and television repairers	338	111
31	Telephone line installers, splicers	396	104	67	Office managers, nec.	337	507
32	Stationary engineers	393	193	68	Estimators and investigators, nec.	337	570
33	Firefighters	393	218	69	Surveyors	336	68
34	Brickmasons and stonemasons	392	144	70	Dispatchers and starters, vehicle	335	110
35	Writers, artists, entertainers, nec.	391	117	71	Bus drivers	332	354
36	Chemical technicians	384	93	72	Truck drivers	330	1841
37	Engineering and science technicians, nec.	380	266				

(continued)

FIGURE 2-1, continued

Earnings in Jobs That Don't Require a College Degree—Continued

Rank and Occupation	1982 Median Weekly Earnings	1982 Employment (thousands)
73 Clinical laboratory technologists and technicians	326	266
74 Radiologic technologists and technicians	325	108
75 Asbestos and insulation workers	323	47
76 Sheriffs and bailiffs	321	77
77 Hucksters and peddlers	320	197
78 Craft and kindred workers, nec.	319	66
79 Meter readers, utilities	317	42
80 Bulldozer operators	317	95
81 Grinding machine operatives	$317	102
82 Dental hygienists	316	58
83 Auto mechanics	307	1034
84 Delivery and route workers	307	574
85 Roofers and slaters	306	133
86 Automobile body repairers	305	197
87 Sales managers, retail trade	302	353

Earnings in Jobs That Don't Require a College Degree—Continued

Rank and Occupation	1982 Median Weekly Earnings	1982 Employment (thousands)
109 Payroll and timekeeping clerks	275	224
110 Warehouse laborers, nec.	275	278
111 Restaurant, cafe, and bar managers	274	768
112 Molders, metal	273	42
113 Statistical clerks	271	365
114 Freight and material handlers	270	696
115 Athletes and kindred workers	269	136
116 Telephone operators	269	283
117 Other office machine operators	261	67
118 Collectors, bill and account	260	87
119 Shipping and receiving clerks	258	499
120 Painters, manufactured articles	258	139
121 Timbercutting and logging workers	257	91
122 Winding operatives, nec.	$256	50
123 Drill press operatives	255	41
124 Practical nurses	255	400

88 Cabinetmakers	302	80
89 Forklift and tow motor operators	301	326
90 Insurance adjusters and examiners	300	200
91 Sales workers, retail trade	298	522
92 Radio operators	296	65
93 Carpet installers	296	85
94 Painters, construction, maintenance	294	472
95 Other health technologists and technicians	293	202
96 Mixing operatives	289	78
97 Miscellaneous machine operatives	288	1153
98 Stock clerks and store keepers	287	497
99 Stenographers	286	66
100 Religious, except clergy	285	61
101 Managers and superintendents, building	285	183
102 Computer and peripheral equipment operators	285	588
103 Secretaries, legal	285	175
104 Checkers, examiners, etc, manufacturing	284	729
105 Other laborers	284	223
106 Punch, stamping press operatives	282	96
107 Meatcutters, butchers, manufacturing	279	93
108 Compositors and typesetters	278	192
125 Construction laborers, except carpenters' helpers	254	735
126 Bottling and canning operatives	253	43
127 Operatives, nec.	248	688
128 Secretaries, medical	247	85
129 Miscellaneous clerical workers, nec.	247	1192
130 Assemblers	246	1087
131 Photographic process workers	245	89
132 Bookkeepers	244	1968
133 Barbers	244	100
134 Enumerators and interviewers	241	53
135 Secretaries, other	241	3587
136 Guards	241	685
137 Library attendants and assistants	240	150
138 Keypunch operators	240	364
139 Taxicab drivers and chauffeurs	240	152
140 Bakers	236	157
141 Upholsterers	236	61
142 Billing clerks	235	154
143 Recreation workers	234	113
144 Filers, polishers, sanders, and buffers	234	113
145 Garbage collectors	233	73
146 Cutting operatives, nec.	232	209

(continued)

FIGURE 2-1, continued

Earnings in Jobs That Don't Require a College Degree—Continued

Rank and Occupation	1982 Median Weekly Earnings	1982 Employment (thousands)
147 Mail handlers, except postal service	229	182
148 Janitors and sextons	229	1406
149 Sawyers	228	112
150 Attendants, personal service, nec.	228	92
151 Typists	227	942
152 Demonstrators	225	116
153 Counter clerks, except food	225	373
154 Newspaper carriers and vendors	223	116
155 Stock handlers	222	972
156 Decorators and window dressers	221	123
157 Housekeepers, except private household	221	182
158 File clerks	220	278
174 Building interior cleaners, nec.	192	926
175 Welfare service aides	190	90
176 Sales clerks, retail trade	188	2447
177 Garage workers and gas station attendants	184	320
178 Farm laborers, wage workers	184	987
179 Nurses' aides and orderlies	182	1136
180 Cooks, except private household	180	1396
181 Laundry and drycleaning operators, nec.	178	188
182 Dressmakers, except factory	177	112
183 Cashiers	176	1683
184 Shoemaking machine operatives	176	72

159 Spinners, twisters, and winders	220	97	185 Clothing ironers and pressers	169	118
160 Health aides, except nursing	219	324	186 Food workers, nec, except private household	169	560
161 Packers and wrappers, except meat and produce	218	582	187 Sewers and stitchers	166	735
162 Carpenters' helpers	$211	51	188 Teachers' aides, except monitors	164	373
163 Gardeners and groundskeepers, except farm	209	722	189 Waiters and waitresses	158	1496
164 Receptionists	207	672	190 Child care workers, except private household	148	472
165 Animal caretakers, except farm	205	101	191 Food counter and fountain workers	145	463
166 Vehicle washers and equipment cleaners	205	183	192 Lodging quarters cleaners, except private household	142	184
167 Messengers and office helpers	204	115	193 Waiters' assistants	140	231
168 Other textile operatives	204	115	194 Dishwashers	140	272
169 Dental assistants	202	151	195 Housekeepers, private household	128	110
170 Bank tellers	199	561	196 Private household cleaners and servants	127	439
171 Hairdressers and cosmetologists	199	573	197 Child care workers, private household	82	469
172 Attendants, recreation and amusement	197	188			
173 Bartenders	196	342			

NOTE: "nec." means not elsewhere classified; "na." means not available.

the point where one-half of the workers earn more and one-half earn less. The list is restricted to occupations with 50,000 or more employees, and self-employment is not included here. Although registered nurses and dental hygienists are noted on this list, keep in mind that many of the jobs in which they are employed require a college degree.

THE SUPER ACHIEVERS AND MONEYMAKERS

Quite apart from these median salaries for the general run of jobs, there are noncollege people who surpass the median in a spectacular way.

For example, there is Barry Diller, hired to head Paramount Pictures at the age of 32 and now, ten years later, chairman and executive officer of the 20th Century-Fox Film Corporation. As reported in "Hollywood's Hottest Stars," an article in *New York Magazine* written by Tony Schwartz, Diller dropped out of the University of California after only a few months in the classroom. At the time he had no real ambitions, but he had a vague leaning toward show business, so he decided, as a first move, to try to get a job in the training program of the William Morris Agency. The agency represented Danny Thomas, and, as Diller grew up with Marlo Thomas, he asked Thomas to intercede to get him an interview. When he was hired, the agency became his alternative education. When he met the head of programming of the American Broadcasting Company, the programming head was so impressed with Diller's knowledge that he offered him a job and, at twenty-three, Diller became assistant to the head of programming.

In that job, Diller's training involved hearing ideas and buying packages of motion pictures. When he suggested that ABC produce its own movies for television and broadcast them each week, he was named to oversee the movies of the week. After nine years at ABC, Diller was offered a chance to become chairman of Paramount Pictures. Ten years later his reported earnings at Paramount were approximately $2.5 million.

When the well-known Mary Kay Ash, one of the most influential and respected personalities in philanthropic and business circles, graduated from high school, there was no money for college so she opted for marriage and children. Later, when the marriage fell apart and she had to make a living, she began as a secretary at a Baptist Church. However, she needed more money than that job paid, so she became a dealer for Stanley Home Products, a direct-sales party plan. Her start was less than auspicious, and she felt totally discouraged when she wanted to attend a company convention but lacked the twelve dollars for train fare to the convention. She borrowed the twelve dollars from a friend, packed her clothes in a Stanley demonstration case, and made the trip. While sitting in the back row at the convention, she took nineteen pages of notes and when the "Queen of Sales" was crowned (a big feature in direct selling) she vowed that she would return the following year and be "Queen of Sales" herself.

Through hard work, she was true to her vow, and ultimately she moved to Dallas where she pursued a 13-year career with Stanley Home Products. Later she was national training director for a company that sold decorative accessories. When she left that job, she began to think about starting her own direct sales company.

Her idea was to sell a beauty product, developed by a woman in Dallas, that she had been using herself for years. After two years of trying, she purchased the product and opened a 500-square-foot shop with a sales staff of nine. Today as chairman of Mary Kay Cosmetics she has a sales force of 194,000 independent beauty consultants. The net sales of $30,000 in 1963 grew to more than $304 million twenty years later.

WHAT ABOUT YOU?

Whether you have super-human ambitions or simply a desire to work at what is right for you, you do not have to be held back in your life unless you allow this yourself—and you do not have to feel inferior to people who have been to college.

Allen Paulson, founder, chairman of the board, and president and chief executive officer of Gulfstream Aerospace Corporation, started to study electrical engineering, but got sidetracked along the way and began working as an aircraft mechanic for thirty cents an hour as an alternative to college.

"You can still get ahead without a degree," he states. "I started with zero and got where I am through hard work and a willingness to take a chance. Know what you are doing and throw a lot of effort into it."

Joseph Nicolato, senior vice president of the Volvo of America Corporation, also feels you can move forward if you give your employer honesty, integrity, and enthusiasm. "If you've made up your mind you're not going to get the four-year degree, those strengths can help compensate," he says.

"A few years ago I said 'Look, Joe, you don't have a college degree—what do you have?'" he revealed. "The answers were *honesty, integrity, dedication, loyalty, initiative,* and *enthusiasm.* And no one ever said you have to have a college degree to have those qualities."

When discussing the number of jobs that are filled by people meeting only some of a job's specifications, Richard Irish, the author of *Go Hire Yourself an Employer,* added, "My advice is to apply for any job you want if you meet half the qualifications."

"When I graduated from high school as valedictorian of my class, I was awarded a year's scholarship to college," declared Barbara Brabec, a home business development specialist, author of *Homemade Money* and *Creative Cash,* and publisher of the National Home Business Report Newsletter. "But I had no interest in going since I wanted to develop skills by working rather than in school. I've never regretted my decision either, and the lack of college never held me back.

"When I went out for what I wanted, I presented myself with such a degree of confidence people never questioned my ability or said 'We can't give you this job because you don't have a college degree.' When people asked if I could do something I'd answer 'Yes, I can' because I've always had a consuming belief that you can do what you want to do. I started with my secretarial skills, and as I've developed other skills, I've always known I could turn a buck in one of a dozen ways. Could a degree in any field offer me the same feeling of security?"

In the final analysis the question "How good will *your* chances be if you don't have a degree?" is answered in this statement by Ronald Kutscher, Associate Commissioner of the Office of Economic Growth and Employment Projections of the Bureau of Labor Statistics. "America's future lies with her high school graduates," says Kutscher. "Most young Americans do not spend four years in college. Many do not spend even a day there and only about one-fourth of 1984's high school graduates are likely to finish college.

"The coming decades will bring challenge and change," continues Kutscher. "We believe, however, that they will offer real opportunity to high school graduates possessing the sound fundamental education that includes the ability to read, write, reason, and compute . . . and the attitudes and personal habits that make for a dependable, responsible, adaptable, and informed worker and citizen."

chapter three

How to Discover What You Want to Do —and What You Can Do

Environmentalist Michael Frome, a nondegree journalist and conservationist who has broken into—and succeeded in—the world of Ph.D.s as a Visiting Associate Professor of Communication and Wildlife Recreation Management at the University of Idaho.

"When I started my working life as a copy boy at the *Washington Post*, I brought in lots of stories and wanted desperately to become a reporter," he said. "But when two jobs opened they were filled by journalism school graduates."

Frome was crushed and went elsewhere. After serving in the military, he returned to the *Post* as a full-fledged reporter writing front-page stories and working without any distinction between him and reporters holding degrees. He had access to higher education under the GI Bill, but when he enrolled at George Washington University for a couple of courses, the courses seemed tame and static compared to his newspaper work.

"Later the American Automobile Association assigned me to develop an anti-billboard legislative and publicity program to protect roadsides from blight," he explained. "I issued materials decrying roadside zoos and soon became interested in national parks. I also developed an expertise in the travel field and got into magazine writing that way. Travel writing led to writing about the environment, and now my passion in life is being involved in trying to save the bits of earth we call parks or wilderness."

We are blessed when we have a passion for our work—and not everyone is that lucky. However, with the right plotting and planning, people at every age and stage can choose job options and lifestyles that will give them personal fulfillment and provide them with what they want out of life. As each of us is different, we cannot all follow the same time frame in deciding what we want. It is still highly desirable to try to find out as early as you can where your best strengths lie and whether you are interested in a job or career that will not require a four-year degree.

This is extremely important as our work shapes our life and lifestyle. In fact, according to John R. Coleman, what we do is so inevitably tied to the person we are that a major part of our self-image is formed by our daily work. In his interview in *Mainliner* magazine, Coleman stated: "To the degree that we are what we do, it becomes all the more important today for each of us to do that which builds upon our own distinctive strengths."

As a result it is never too early, nor too late, to start evaluating what you want and can do so you can embark on a work plan that will make you the kind of person you are capable of becoming.

TAKING STOCK

The next few pages of soul-searching will provide you with a free flow of ideas that you can combine with other tools to decide what you want to do. You may feel confused occasionally and have conflicts within yourself. But it is normal to have that problem at first, and it will disappear as you get signals that show you choices that will enrich you life.

You will find that some of the paperwork will sometimes seem to repeat itself and encourage similar answers. This is as it should be. The exercises are planned for that.

START A JOURNAL

Get a looseleaf notebook in which to (1) record the feelings, attitudes, emotions, and thoughts you experience each day and (2) write your answers (a few at a time) to the questions listed below. Take as long as you need on each one.

What is your definition of success?
What kind of lifestyle do you want?
What were your best subjects in school?

What have school experiences, activities in clubs, leisure pursuits, and volunteer work shown that you are good at?

What is your part-time or full-time work history so far?

What is your idea of a *good* job—the kind you would most like to have?

Will your answer to the foregoing pay your rent or mortgage; fulfill your needs and desires; and hold your ongoing interest?

What kind of work can you obtain now that would point you in the direction of the work you want?

If you could have any job of your choice what would you want the most at the moment?

Are you most successful working with ideas or things?

If with ideas, what kind of creativity and self-expression do you use? If with things, do you lean toward construction, design, or repair?

How much money do you want to earn and how important is the size of your paycheck as a measure of how you value yourself?

Do you need immediate gratification from your work or can you accept a slow start?

Are you willing to make sacrifices and take risks in order to get what you want?

If you are working now, how good are your chances of advancement?

How energetic, assertive, and positive are you?

Do you enjoy challenge and competition?

Do you like setting goals and surpassing them?

Do you have support and encouragement from people whose lives are connected to yours?

Working conditions on a job can add or detract from job satisfaction, so take the following test for this and check your answers in the boxes.

WHERE would you like to work?
- ☐ outdoors
- ☐ inside
- ☐ in a quiet place
- ☐ in a busy place
- ☐ in one building
- ☐ moving around the city
- ☐ traveling around the country—or the world
- ☐ near your house
- ☐ far away from home

WHEN would you like to work?
- ☐ the same days each week
- ☐ different days each week
- ☐ regular hours
- ☐ changing hours
- ☐ daytime only
- ☐ at night

HOW do you like to work?
- ☐ at new or different tasks each day
- ☐ at the same tasks each day
- ☐ by yourself
- ☐ with a few other people
- ☐ with lots of other people
- ☐ dressed up
- ☐ in casual clothes
- ☐ sitting down
- ☐ moving around

**Reprinted by permission from
Suit Youself, Wider
Opportunities for Women**

WRITE YOUR AUTOBIOGRAPHY

At the John C. Crystal Center for Creative Life/Work Planning, participants are asked to write detailed autobiographies, outlining not just their work experiences but all their life experiences. The purpose is to find out not whether they have a degree in a particular area but whether they can actually function in a particular area.

Crystal proposes you begin your autobiography by

imagining your life in chapters that represent the various time periods of your life to date. Note how you became involved in the activities mentioned in each chapter. Write what you did in each activity and how you feel about the involvement.

After you have written at least part of your autobiography Crystal recommends getting a supply of small white index cards. As you read each page of your autobiography note in a few words on the cards what skill you employed. Then compare the cards from your work and leisure activities and from the early and later stages of your life. Crystal believes that in this way you can find skills that permeate many activites and cut across the boundaries of time. Group your demonstrated skills into "clusters" that relate to each other. From these categories select eight or ten clusters as possible skills to use and develop.

Some questions Crystal suggests asking are:

- What turns you off or on?
- What bores, excites, intrigues, angers you?
- What people make you feel comfortable/uncomfortable?
- What kinds of communities would you be happiest living in?
- What would you like your friends to remember you for?

Along with enabling you to get a picture of your likes, your autobiography will show you some things you have done that you do not want to do anymore.

WORK QUALITIES

Circle the qualities in which you feel strong, and check those in which you feel weak.

Work Qualities

1. I have adequate education or training.
2. I can accept responsibility.
3. I can accept criticism.
4. I am not overly shy or self-conscious.
5. I will be willing to move if the job requires it.
6. I can get along with most of the people I meet.
7. I like to work alone, without supervision.
8. I do not mind some repetitious work.
9. I can get other people to cooperate in a task.
10. I like to be part of a team.
11. I do not try to dominate others.
12. I believe that I can cope with most problems if I have enough time.
13. I do not hate, reject or pass judgment on others just because they are different.
14. Helping other people makes me feel good.
15. I believe that I can bring good qualities to my job.
16. I want to get ahead in my job.
17. I do not disregard the rights of others.
18. I like to see the physical results of my work.
19. I like the freedom of using my own ideas.
20. I would rather be told what to do and have someone oversee my work.

Reprinted by permission from
Self Evaluation Career Guide,
Pilot Books

FEELING GOOD

List ten things you have done, and are doing, that have made you feel happy and satisfied. Rate them 1 through 10 and examine them for common threads.

10. _____
9. _____
8. _____
7. _____

6. _____
5. _____
4. _____
3. _____
2. _____
1. _____

WHO AM I?—AGAIN

By now this potpourri of paperwork should be pointing to concrete answers to that question "Who am I?" Taking your cue from the exercises you have done write five specific answers to the question "Who am I?"

1. _____
2. _____
3. _____
4. _____
5. _____

AND NOW—FANTASYLAND

After this trip into realism, you are entitled to daydream a bit, and there is current support for this in the career counseling field.

As a starter, one well-known and respected person, John L. Holland, professor of social relations and psychology at the John Hopkins University and author of *Making Vocational Choices: A Theory of Careers,* believes daydreams can be an excellent guide. He asks people to list their occupational daydreams, favorite activities, and special competences. Then, with the aid of an Occupational Finder, they can come up with a list of occupations.

Two other researchers—Dr. Thomas Skovholt, professor of social and behavioral sciences at the University of Minnesota, and Dr. James Morgan, counseling psychologist at the University of Florida Counseling Center—have found that both spontaneous and guided fantasies can provide worthwhile information in career counseling.

"Daydreams can be very valuable in helping people find directions in the choice of a career and, also, along the course of their career development," stresses Skovholt.

In their work with spontaneous fantasy, the researchers stimulate imagination with such questions as:

What occupations do you fantasize or daydream about now?

As a child, what were your occupational daydreams and how do you feel about these daydreams today?

What kind of work seems to be excluded from your fantasies or daydreams?

In their guided fantasy approach, Skovholt and Morgan lead people through a relaxation process before asking them to imagine a typical day in the future by letting images form in their minds as counselors ask such questions as:

How do you get to work?

How do things look along the way?

What do you notice when you get to you workplace?

What do you feel as you enter?

Who else is there?

Do you stay in or go out for lunch?

Are you alone or with someone?

What is the last thing you do before you get ready to quit for the day?

What does your home look like?

Who, if anyone, is with you for your evening meal?

What do you do in the evening?

What pleased you in particular about your day?

"Perhaps the most difficult part of using the fantasy experience for the first time is just being willing to give it a try . . . to suspend disbelief and go with the experience," says Morgan. "Those who do are often amazed and pleased at how rich and full their fantasy is."

YOU'RE NOT FINISHED YET

Now that you are getting to know yourself, there are several more things that you can do to help you choose the work and lifestyle that will give you what you want. The following is a general overview. Each suggestion will be expanded in the subsequent chapters.

1. Follow Your Natural Talents as Much as You Can

As a child Joseph De Sio was fascinated by machinery. He later followed this natural inclination to a job as a temporary relief helper in the engineering department at Rockefeller Center in Manhattan. Today he is supervisor of engineering maintenance for all departments of the complex, and this responsibility includes not only building maintenance but also maintenance of plumbing, steam lines, gas lines, steam machines, vacuums, snow equipment, and valves.

"While going to school I used to work in factories on Saturdays hanging around machines observing, learning, and helping," explained De Sio. "Then after a stint in the service I worked at a variety of jobs with mechanics. During this time a friend mentioned jobs for mechanics at Rockefeller Center and suggested I apply. When I followed his advice I obtained the temporary relief helper's job."

When an opening to transfer to mechanical work came, De Sio switched to that. After some time as a maintenance mechanic, he was promoted to assistant supervisor of engineering maintenance.

"When I started out I learned primarily through reading and on the job experience," he said. "When a machine would come in I'd get the catalog that came with it, with its breakdown of pictures, and study and learn that way. I also went to electrical trade school to expand my background and knowledge."

It is great when, like De Sio, your natural inclinations show early. But this does not happen for everyone who ultimately finds the right option.

How to Discover What You Want to Do

"In my case, there was no sign until I went to photography school that I had a natural bent for this field, and even when I was involved enough to do photographs I could show my instructor I didn't see any handwriting on the wall," admits Jean Deer. "As far as I could see I was just enjoying the work. Because I liked taking pictures, I'd photograph people's children and as people saw the work I did they encouraged me to go into business.

"I didn't know exactly where I wanted to go, so I just started from the beginning and kept going," he acknowledged. "Since I had no studio in which to work, I had to go outdoors to photograph people until I could open a studio in my home. The outdoor photography that became a specialty had its roots in this need."

2. Consider Tests to Get a Peg on Your Interests and Ability if Your Natural Inclination Does Not Give You Clues and Your Self-Evaluation Findings Still Need an Extra Boost

Not all career specialists believe in tests, but it is possible that interest and aptitude tests may be helpful to you. Many State Employment Agencies and service organizations, such as YMCAs, provide a certain amount of career guidance and counseling. So do high school guidance counselors and counseling offices at community and other colleges. Private counseling and career development services offer vocational interest tests such as the Kuder Occupational Interest Survey and the Strong-Campbell Interest Inventory. Qualified counselors can interpret the results, talk over various potentials, and discuss whether you are qualified for work that matches your interest. You should always be aware, however, that *no* tests can give you absolute answers. They are only a tool.

3. Talk to People and Follow Their Examples

By asking people the right questions you will learn about the positives and negatives of a job field; people's personal experiences; exactly what they do; how they got their first job; how they progressed from that beginning; and how they like or dislike their work.

"When you mingle with a lot of people it draws you out of yourself and makes you voice your inner dreams and ambitions," maintains Barbara Brabec, the home business development specialist. "Once you voice your ambitions you're more able to pursue the road you must take."

The road that Barbara took began with part-time jobs in high school and ten years of post-high school office jobs. "The lack of a college degree never held me back from well-paying jobs or promotions," she advised. "Through reading and talking to people I'd identify with those persons and think 'I could do that.'"

This faith in herself, along with her consuming interest in handcrafts, led Barbara into starting a magazine *Artisan Crafts*, which she published with the help of her husband for five years. Although neither knew anything about writing or publishing, Barbara studied and expanded her knowledge. She also developed and maintained mailing lists; planned bulk promotional mailings; created direct mail pieces; and compiled two editions of a national crafts directory. When a mutual friend told a publisher about her work, the publisher asked Barbara to write *Creative Cash*. As the book neared publication, the publisher suggested that Barbara come into the office to work for him on a part-time basis as his assistant. Later, when the publisher was killed in an airline crash, Barbara—without a college degree—became publisher and general manager of the book publishing company.

"While I held that job I launched my newsletter on home businesses and crafts, planning to do it evenings and weekends," she said. "But before too long I realized I could not continue to work full-time as a book publisher and also make the kind of gains I wanted to make in the crafts field as a writer, lecturer, and self-publisher so I left the publishing company and launched myself as an entrepreneur. College would have done nothing for me. I'm self-taught, and this is what led me to where I am today."

How to Discover What You Want to Do

4. Try Working in Temporary Jobs in Fields That Interest You

"In a temporary job you're in a front row seat to see much that happens in business," says William Olsten, chairman of the board of The Olsten Corporation, a nationwide temporary service. "You never know what a business is like until you get in there and see it, so a person who covers a variety of assignments over a period of time can conceivably find an industry that fits his or her interests and talents."

When you register with a temporary service, a service representative will determine your skills, availability, and areas of interest. A good service will try, as much as possible, to send you on assignments that match your interests, although none can guarantee this, as everything depends on client orders. As you take jobs, keep your eyes open; ask questions that help you learn; absorb what you can from your supervisors; note requirements for entry-level positions in fields that interest you; and observe the upward-mobility routes.

5. Do Volunteer and Community Work

This can be an excellent way to discover more of your interests; develop work-related skills; and make valuable social and business contacts

"It also show you're a responsible person concerned with making contributions in your away-from-work-time," says Charlene Margaritis, who started in the fashion industry and who now has an executive level career in advertising and public relations.

"I left college after one year because my family moved from one area to another," she declared. "At first I intended to continue, but since I was anxious to start working, my alternative was looking for a job in the fashion field since my family was involved in that and I knew something about it."

While Charlene got her feet wet in business and kept her eyes open for good opportunities, she devoted a good portion of her spare time to civic and charitable work. "As

FIGURE 3-1

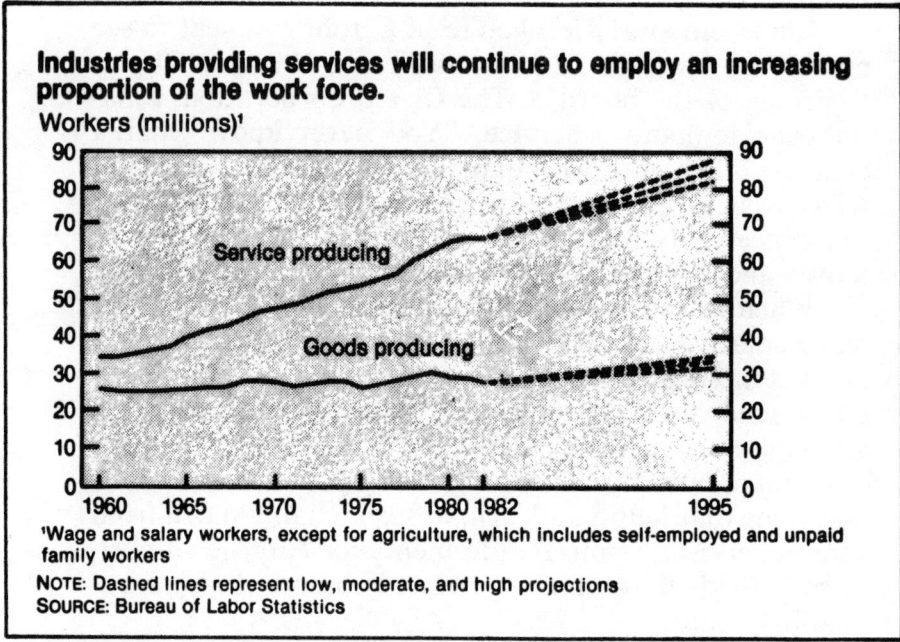

a result, I got a lot of exposure to all different kinds of people in all different facets of business. I made good contacts on a business level, and I highly recommend this approach."

6. Learn What the Employment Prospects Are

It is foolish to set your sights on a field that went out with high button shoes, so investigate what is out there. (See Chapters Four and Five). Figures 3-1 and 3-2 provide a concise picture of employment prospects through this decade.

7. Find Out What Training is Necessary

There is post-high school training for almost any work, so ambitious people who know what they want can obtain post-high school training in many different ways. (See Chapter Seven for alternatives.)

FIGURE 3-2

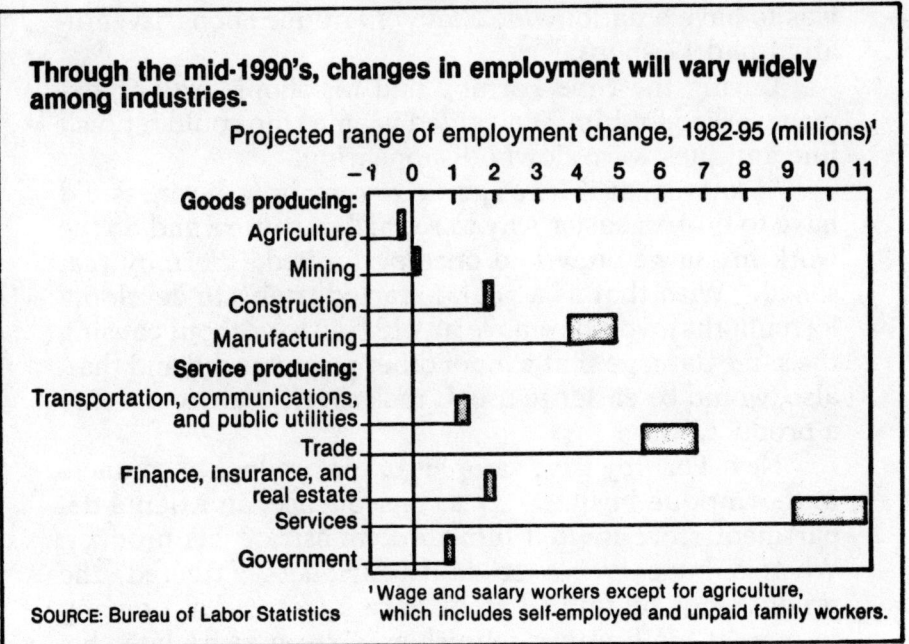

For one example of an alternative, take the case of Homer Formby, the country's best-known authority on refinishing and caring for fine wood. When Formby was only 8 years old he started working after school in his father's antique and refinishing shop.

"As time went on my father taught me more and more," stated Formby, "So when I got out of school I felt I didn't need a college education. Instead of spending four years in college I wanted to get on to a good, sound business."

To do this Formby went to New York in 1946 to work with one of the best woodcarvers in the country.

"I worked with him all day for 1½ years for $25 a week," he recalled. "At night I worked till 11:00 p.m. in a restaurant because I couldn't live on $25 a week. Next I went to Cincinnati to work with a master in inlaying and other fine techniques. When I returned south my ambition was to have a nationwide chain of antique shops. Eventually I had 17 shops."

During the time Formby had his shops forty craftsmen worked for him. But skilled people who could refinish fine antiques were slowly disappearing.

"I knew that if I was going to remain in business, I'd have to find an easier way to refinish furniture and do the work my large crew had once performed," Formby reasoned. "With that as a goal, I started trying to develop a formula that would remove an old finish, without causing the same damage that a lot of other products did and that, also, would be easier to use. It took seven years to develop a product."

Next Formby gave samples of his product to contacts in the antique business. As a consequence, an Atlanta department store invited him to demonstrate his product. When a huge crowd of do-it-yourselfers gathered, the product took off immediately. Formby formed a company to market his funiture refinisher. Sixteen years later his products line the shelves of more than thirty thousand home centers and hardware stores.

"A college degree is for some people—but definitely not for everyone," believes Formby. "I know that I probably would have not been as successful as I have been if I had gone to college. I constantly get letters and resumes from people who have college degrees who aren't happy with what they're doing and who are searching for something better."

8. Expect to be Flexible

The one sure thing in life is change, so you need sufficient flexibility to accommodate quick shifts in jobs.

Joseph Meister, president and chief operating officer of House of Bread—a thriving and growing enterprise in which he sells frozen bread dough to supermarkets, delicatessens, and convenience stores to be baked on the premises as customers watch—is a story of flexibility in searching for the right work.

How to Discover What You Want to Do

While mowing lawns during his school years, Meister noticed his customers with money lived a lot better than his family. When he got out of school his goal was to be a millionaire. "I had no idea how it would all come together," he reported. "But I knew it would."

Getting it together included a job as a "go-fer" in a woodworking factory; spending time in his father's brake lining factory; opening a delicatessen; making a false start in the bread-and-butter pickle business; and running an industrial catering service.

"I had six catering trucks," announced Meister. "But I knew nothing about the business so I lost a lot of money in less than six months time. I didn't go bankrupt, though. Instead I called my creditors and promised if they'd be patient I'd pay them 100 cents for the dollar. I did it, too. But it took three years."

One of the persons to whom Meister owed money was a baker and one day while Meister was in the bakery he noticed bread dough in the baker's freezer. The baker explained he made the dough ahead of time and baked it off on weekends because he could not make it fast enough then. Meister thought, "I can do that" and immediately began to picture a vast freezer full of nothing but bread dough waiting to be delivered to stores and baked and sold on the premises.

"I had a commercial piece of property next to a cemetery," Meister remembers, "so I began with that rent-free store and a $70,000 line of credit from my baker friend. Until I could get equipment I made a proof box to raise the bread out of my wife's electric frying pan."

The success of Meister's first store prompted him to expand and now he has over 100 locations and is busy making his million in rye rather than ROM's. He is another proof that when you are able to find what you want, the "can do" will bring you along.

MAYBE YOU WOULD LIKE TO BE YOUR OWN BOSS

"When you don't have a college degree, I believe the type of person most likely to succeed is the entrepreneurial type," says Madame Wellington who is known for designing and marketing "fabulous fake" counterfeit diamonds that rival the beauty of real gems.

As one of the country's outstanding examples of entrepreneurship Madame Wellington (Helen Ver Standig) has had her achievements recognized and honored by the coveted Joseph Wharton Award, presented to her by the Wharton School Club of Washington. Despite the fact that she has no degree, she also teaches marketing at the prestigious Wharton School.

"Even though I lecture at the Wharton School I feel very strongly that college isn't for everyone," she said, "and even if I'd had the option of going I'm not sure I'd have been college material when I started working at age 16. While in high school I had a part-time job selling classified advertising. Later this got me started selling advertising on a full-time basis for the Washington newspaper where I met my husband."

The Ver Standigs' first venture together was beginning weekly newspapers in Rhode Island and South Carolina. Later their entrepreneurial spirit led them into opening an advertising agency in the Washington, D.C. area. After 25 successful years in advertising, the couple gave up that business and looked for new ventures in which to invest their money. One venture became the counterfeit diamonds that Madame Wellington (her husband's name for her) learned about when she met a laser scientist who was trying to develop simulated diamonds with a chemical formula. He needed $10,000 to continue his work so Madame put up the money.

Subsequently, she received a packet of diamonds in the mail, and when market research convinced her that Wellington diamonds would fill a need, she found jewelers who could replicate the settings of Harry Winston and Cartier and started her business on a mail order basis. Soon sales were so successful that retail stores were opened in key cities throughout the country.

Many people share her view that the type of person

most likely to succeed without a college degree is the entrepreneurial type.

"I think not having a degree is being overcome more and more through entrepreneurship," stresses Howard Shenson, a consulting specialist who holds seminars around the country for aspiring and practicing consultants. "The growth in entrepreneurship is reflective of the way people are overcoming the 'piece of paper' barrier."

Current studies show that people who become entrepreneurs choose this alternative because they have a strong need to achieve; a fierce drive for independence; a desire for job satisfaction that they cannot get in other ways; and—sometimes—the economic need to take this route.

WHAT ARE THE ODDS FOR SUCCESS IN ENTREPRENEURSHIP?

Despite the foregoing lures and promises, the odds against success are enormous. According to the United States Small Business Administration, it is difficult to collect hard-core data on business failures. The failure rate is very high and reportedly 65 percent of all new businesses fail within the first five years. More that ten thousand businesses fold each year. Dun and Bradstreet, Inc., the oldest and probably the most prestigious of the business information service companies, has documented during the past several years that over ninety percent of business failures are due to managerial inexperience or ineptitude. Other major reasons are undercapitalization and inadequate preparation.

"Another fatal error is attempting to start a business without adequately assesssing you own personality," adds Edward Nepkie, a business professor at United States International University in San Diego. "It's all wrapped up in one word—DRIVE. You need to have a commitment to succeed and a willingness to work hard."

ASSESSING YOUR PERSONALITY FOR ENTREPRENEURSHIP

Although every person who starts a business does not have *every* personality trait and *every* qualification to succeed, you will need a good number of the qualities noted in the following questions.

Answer each one with a check mark (√) under YES or NO

	YES	NO
1. Are you a good organizer?		
2. Are you a good salesperson?		
3. Do you have good communication skills?		
4. Are you knowledgeable about the product or service you'd like to offer?		
5. Do you have a strong belief in yourself and your abilities?		
6. Do you have a confident and authoritative manner?		
7. Are you at least a little experienced in business and management?		
8. Does competition spur you on to push toward your goals even harder?		
9. Can you think things through and be decisive?		
10. Do you have plenty of stamina and spunk?		

Count your check marks (√) in each column. If a large percentage come under YES your chance of success will undoubtedly be good. If they are evenly divided, think twice about giving up a paycheck for self-employment. If they are overwhelmingly NO, forget about going into business.

If your chances of success are good and you are enthusiastic about entrepreneurship, take the "Entrepreneur" test (Figure 3-3) created by Gladys W. Hudson. It is included here with the permission of *The Executive Female*, a publication of the National Association for Female Executives, 120 E. 56th St., New York, NY 10022 (212)371-0740. The statements apply to both men and women.

One person who might have scored high on this test is

FIGURE 3-3

Should You Be An Entrepreneur?

Circle the number after each statement that best indicates the accuracy of the statement as a description of you.

	Highly Accurate		Completely Inaccurate
1. I am a "take charge" person; I like to control what happens.		5 4 3 2 1	
2. I see situations in their broadest aspects and their fullest complexities.		5 4 3 2 1	
3. I feel exhilarated when facing obstacles or problems.		5 4 3 2 1	
4. I am a leader of people.		5 4 3 2 1	
5. I feel comfortable delegating work to others and accepting reasonable success—even though I would have handled the project differently.		5 4 3 2 1	
6. I assess my abilities realistically.		5 4 3 2 1	
7. I can ask for and accept help or advice in areas outside my special expertise.		5 4 3 2 1	
8. I exercise initiative and accept responsibility for my own activity.		5 4 3 2 1	
9. I set my own activity level and deadlines rather than waiting for others to impose them.		5 4 3 2 1	
10. I am thorough and accurate in accomplishing any project I undertake.		5 4 3 2 1	
11. I manage my finances according to a predetermined plan.		5 4 3 2 1	
12. I enjoy the thrill of taking calculated risks.		5 4 3 2 1	
13. I have the emotional ability to			

(continued)

FIGURE 3-3, continued

bounce back after failure or temporary set-backs.	5 4 3 2 1
14. I have the "staying power" that enables me to keep at a project in spite of discouragements, delays or disappointments.	5 4 3 2 1
15. I am willing to devote to my business whatever amount of time, energy, or other resources might be required for success.	5 4 3 2 1
16. I am willing to seek and accept the obligations of outside financing.	5 4 3 2 1
17. I want to achieve financial independence.	5 4 3 2 1

Add all the numbers you circled. The highest possible figure is 85. If you scored at least 70, operating your own business fits many of your priorities. A high rating is especially important for items 12 through 16.

doll clothes designer Fay Mitzner. Her company, Originals by Fay, Ltd., designs and manufactures a fine line of doll clothes. She is also a consultant for a manufacturer of doll accessories and, because of her knowledge and experience, she has given seminars at New York's Fashion Institute of Technology.

"If you look at my grade school album where it says 'What do you what to be?' you'd see that I wrote 'Designer,'" she said. "Then in high school I had an excellent design course and a teacher who encouraged me. She'd always say she had other students who had more talent than I but none who showed such tenacity and determination. As soon as I graduated I took any work I could find to get started."

One of Fay's first jobs was finishing seams for a fashionable Fifth Avenue store. Next she did display work that led to doing miniature designs for a pattern firm. She was then hired by a sewing machine company to research the gowns of the Ladies of the White House and create replicas for dolls displayed at a New York World's Fair.

Before her first entrepreneurial venture—a children's retail clothing shop which she ran with her husband—Fay went on to design children's clothing for manufacturers. When her husband died, she sold their shop and established her present business. Her advice to entrepreneurs is to decide what you want to do, and then go after it. For steps to take to "go after it" see the Resource Directory for titles of books on starting a business and for names of helpful organizations.

II

HUNDREDS OF JOBS FOR THE NON-COLLEGE GRADUATE

chapter four

Job Opportunities in the Trades, the Arts, and the Office . . .

Arthur Leavitt was a machinist in 1961, and Crystal, his wife, was a high school dropout who had never worked. With their infant daughter, Shelly, they lived on fifty-five dollars a week in an unheated apartment where they stuffed newspapers into the windows to keep out the cold and cooked with an electric frying pan because they had no stove.

Today they are successful executives with Lady Finelle Cosmetics, an international direct sales company. In their early 40s they could easily retire—if they did not prefer to continue as vice-presidents of marketing responsible for a salesforce of 11,000 people. "If anybody told us 23 years ago that we would be so successful we would have laughed," Crystal said.

Arthur agrees that at the time Crystal started selling, their only thought was that selling would bring in some money and give Crystal more confidence in herself. Two years later she was doing so well that Arthur quit his machinist's job to join her business.

"After dropping out of high school I never thought I'd accomplish anything," Crystal admitted. "But, without a college degree, direct sales has provided me with confidence and self-worth."

There are many other good occupations that don't need a four-year degree, and the table in Figure 4-1 pinpoints forty with the largest job growth projected for 1982-95. Only a handful require four years of college training.

HELP WANTED: MEN AND WOMEN

Most of the jobs for the future are open to both men and women, and although the skilled trades are not for every woman, many, for their own reasons, are moving away from lower-level, lower-income white and pink collar jobs to go into the trades. In some situations they are also moving up to supervisory and management spots.

In one case, a 33-year-old carpenter held a variety of office jobs before she applied for an apprenticeship in the

Job Opportunities

FIGURE 4-1

Forty occupations with largest job growth, 1982–95

Occupation	Change in total employment (in thousands)	Percent of total job growth	Percent change
Building custodians	779	3.0	27.5
Cashiers	744	2.9	47.4
Secretaries	719	2.8	29.5
General clerks, office	696	2.7	29.6
Salesclerks	685	2.7	23.5
Nurses, registered	642	2.5	48.9
Waiters and waitresses	562	2.2	33.8
Teachers, kindergarten and elementary	511	2.0	37.4
Truckdrivers	425	1.7	26.5
Nursing aides and orderlies	423	1.7	34.8
Sales representatives, technical	386	1.5	29.3
Accountants and auditors	344	1.3	40.2
Automotive mechanics	324	1.3	38.3
Supervisors of blue-collar workers	319	1.2	26.6
Kitchen helpers	305	1.2	35.9
Guards and doorkeepers	300	1.2	47.3
Food preparation and service workers, fast food restaurants	297	1.2	36.7
Managers, store	292	1.1	30.1
Carpenters	247	1.0	28.6
Electrical and electronic technicians	222	.9	60.7
Licensed practical nurses	220	.9	37.1
Computer systems analysts	217	.8	85.3
Electrical engineers	209	.8	65.3
Computer programmers	205	.8	76.9
Maintenance repairers, general utility	193	.8	27.8
Helpers, trades	190	.7	31.2
Receptionists	189	.7	48.8
Electricians	173	.7	31.8
Physicians	163	.7	34.0
Clerical supervisors	162	.6	34.6
Computer operators	160	.6	75.8
Sales representatives, nontechnical	160	.6	27.4
Lawyers	159	.6	34.3
Stock clerks, stockroom and warehouse	156	.6	18.8
Typists	155	.6	15.7
Delivery and route workers	153	.6	19.2
Bookkeepers, hand	152	.6	15.9
Cooks, restaurants	149	.6	42.3
Bank tellers	142	.6	30.0
Cooks, short order, specialty and fast food	141	.6	32.2

Note: Includes only detailed occupations with 1982 employment of 25,000 or more. Data for 1995 are based on moderate-trend projections.

SOURCE: Bureau of Labor Statistics

carpentry trade. "I like working with my hands, and I like working outside, even though it can be tough when the weather is cold," she commented.

When she started many of her male co-workers were sure she would soon give up. "They couldn't believe me," she recalled. "But I came back day after day. Later as they saw I was really working the novelty wore off."

In another instance a woman who had always loved cars landed in the parts department of a car sales and service agency—after spending two years in college and trying several different jobs. She had natural mechanical ability, so she gradually learned to make car repairs by watching the mechanics work. Subsequently this experience, plus other jobs in the automotive industry, led to a spot as an assistant service manager in a good-sized automobile agency. In her job, she assisted in running the shop; ordered gasoline, tools, and equipment; kept up to date on all requirements and aspects of cars; and worked on actual repairs.

TAKE YOUR CHOICE!
HERE IS THE WHOLE WORLD OF OPTIONS!

As previous chapters have indicated, the majority of noncollege graduates will have to settle for entry level jobs and plan to build from there. However, as we have also seen previously, many people with four-year degrees must start at this level too, and they often have to acquire specialized training in order to get a job. Some specialized training is always a plus, when you are ready to market yourself. While you are acquiring a specialty broaden your general education, too, as this will enable you to change as the world and technology change.

Frequently the best opportunities for people without a four-year degree are in smaller institutions rather than large corporations. To back that up, government statistics show that 80 percent of all new hirings are in companies with 20 employees or less. Adds counselor John C. Crystal: "These jobs are less likely to fall victim to automation since they are usually multifaceted rather than highly specialized, as in the larger companies."

Detailed information on every job option cannot be covered in a single chapter (or even a single book) so the sampling of options that is listed in this and the following chapter is only the initial step in researching many choices. You will find there is some overlapping as some jobs fit more than one field. Also be sure to keep in mind that each listing is only a representative sample. There are many other jobs.

As you spot fields that interest you, turn to the Resource Directory for names of organizations that can give you in-depth descriptions of (1) jobs within each field; (2) what people do in each job; (3) qualifications and training needed; (4) places of employment; and (5) working conditions.

Chapter Seven will discuss training and Chapter Two has already provided median earnings for jobs without college. Refer to that for a general idea of what people can expect to earn. But keep the word "median" in your mind and remember that top-level earners (like many of the men and women in this book) are those who pass the "median" criterion in their approach to their work. Lists of the main job fields follow. In addition to the suggestions here, there is a vast array of other choices that people enter through a side door when they do not have a four-year degree.

SKILLED TRADES AND CRAFTS

As equipment used by industry and consumers becomes increasingly complex, skilled trades and crafts promise continued growth, although some some jobs will grow more rapidly than others. Just as one example, automotive mechanics are projected to grow about 38 percent from 1982 to 1995 and add nearly 324,000 jobs to the field.

Because the majority of crafts and skilled trades are heavily unionized, they generally offer the highest earnings in industrial employment below the management level. With the exception of management jobs and professions, such as medicine and law, skilled mechanics and craftspersons frequently have earnings comparable to many white-collar jobs.

In the electrical industry, for instance, A. J. Phillips, Director of the National Joint Apprenticeship and Training Committee for the Electrical Industry reports: "The four-year apprenticeship training program for the Electrical Construction Industry is roughly equivalent to an Associate Degree and upon completion entitles the individual to journeyman status where salaries range from $30,000 and up."

Some of the Jobs

Air conditioning, refrigeration and heating mechanics
Aircraft mechanics
Airplane mechanics
Assemblers
Automobile body repairers
Automobile mechanics
Automobile painters
Automobile trimmers & installers
Blacksmiths
Boat motor mechanics
Bookbinders
Bowling pin machine mechanics
Brake operators and couplers
Bricklayers
Bridge and building workers
Building custodians
Building inspectors
Carpenters
Cement masons
Compositors
Construction machinery operators
Coremakers
Diesel mechanics
Electricians
Electric sign repairers
Electrotypers and stereotypers
Elevator constructors
Farm equipment mechanics
Firefighters
Floor covering installers
Fork lift technicians
Forgeshop workers
Furniture upholsterers
Glaziers
Guards
Gasoline service station attendants

Industrial machinery repairers
Instrument makers
Insulation workers
Iron workers
Latherers
Line installation & cable splicers
Lithographers
Locksmiths
Locomotive engineers
Locomotive firemen
Machinists Machine Tool operators
Manufacturing inspectors
Marble setters
Metalcutters
Millwrights
Molders
Motorcycle mechanics
Operating Engineer
Painters
Paperhangers
Pattern makers
Pest controllers
Photographers
Pipefitters
Plasterers
Plumbers
Power truck operators
Printers
Printing press operators
Proofreaders
Roofers
Sheet metal workers
Shipping and receiving clerks
Signal department workers
Stationary engineers
Stock clerks
Stone masons
Structural, ornamental, and reinforcing iron workers, riggers and machine movers
Telephone installers & repairers
Tool and die makers
Truck & bus mechanics
Typesetters
Vending machine mechanics
Waste water treatment plant operators
Welders

THE GLAMOUR INDUSTRIES: ART, CREATIVE CRAFTS, COMMUNICATIONS, ENTERTAINMENT

Because of the emphasis on talent, rigid academic qualifications are not always required for the so-called "glamour" jobs. You do not need a degree, for example, to be a writer, artist, entertainer, or performer. However, you will have stiff competition and, along with a strong artistic talent, you will need creativity, ambition, discipline, drive, stamina, tenacity, and originality. Above all, you will need the confidence to keep going when the disappointments come. But as a balance to rejections there are many exhilarating "highs."

"I decided not to complete college when I realized that what I wanted to do didn't require that I be there any longer," said Duncan Cleary, a 31-year-old guitarist, songwriter, and recording artist. "I still have a lot to learn about music. But in terms of being in a structured situation it was time to move on and get involved in the field itself. Consequently, I just threw myself into my own training.

"I got started by playing in local bars and similar establishments," he explained. "Then I got into recording because I had some friends who were recording engineers in New York. As I met more and more people I gradually got to places like Avery Fisher Hall in Lincoln Center.

"Not having a degree has never been a problem," he contended. "You have to be able to play well, of course. But if you have the right personality and expose your work to many people, the diploma won't make any difference."

Richard Leech, a youthful tenor in New York's City Opera, has also found not having a degree is in no way affecting his progress.

A native of Binghamton, New York, he went to Eastman at the University of Rochester for exactly one semester. He realized almost immediately that he preferred the musical training he had received in Binghamton at the Tri-Cities Opera Company. When he left college after such a short time, it was difficult for his parents to understand. However, they accepted his decision as long as he supported himself, which he did by working in restaurants.

His choice was obviously the right one because, Leech, in his late twenties, is well on his way to becoming a star in an operatic career. "Everthing I learned about opera," he revealed in an interview for *The New York Times* "comes from actually trying it out in Binghamton, New York."

Public relations is a "glamour" field that traditionally asks for a four-year degree. But as you have seen (and will see) in these pages many nondegree people succeed in this work.

"Overcoming not having that 'piece of paper' is done by hard work and showing employers that you are dedicated to getting the job done and doing it well," says publicist Diane Hannan who, at age 28, began her own public relations firm with the famous Lake Placid Resort Hotel as her first client. "To date I have not outwardly experienced any problems without a degree. But you do have to have a great deal of confidence and continually educate yourself. College is no guarantee."

Some of the Jobs

Actors and Actresses
Advertising personnel
Batik designers
Broadcasters
Cabinetmakers
Candlemakers
Cartoonists
Ceramicists
Clowns
Commercial artists
Dancers
Entertainers
Fashion designers
Floral designers
Furniture makers & refinishers
Glass blowers
Graphic artists
Jewelry designers
Leather workers
Metalworkers
Models
Musicians
Photographers
Potters
Public Relations practitioners
Puppeteers
Radio and TV personalities
Silk screeners
Singers
Stained glass artists
Theatre set designers
Weavers
Wood carvers
Writers

PARAPROFESSIONALS

Paraprofessionals are well-trained people who relieve professionals (with four-year and advanced degrees) of many of their tasks. But as a paraprofessional you are spared the long preparation professionals have to have, while at the same time, you work in their fields. Most of the time you work in health; physical and life sciences; or law.

In science, paraprofessionals help scientists evaluate processes, analyze data, and prepare tests and experiments under controlled conditions. Training for such work is given by schools of technology, technical institutes, and two-year colleges.

In law, paralegals or legal assistants work under the supervision of lawyers and relieve lawyers of paperwork, legwork, liaison, and other details of investigation and factual research. Although many paralegal jobs require a four-year degree, there is still no hard-and-fast consensus within the profession about the required education. At the present time some people enter with a high school diploma and a paralegal course (accredited by the American Bar Association) that is offered by a law institute or community college.

Some of the Jobs

Agricultural technicians
Biology technicians
Chemical technicians
Earth science technicians
Geology technicians
Hydrologic technicians
Life science technicians
Library technicians and assistants
Meterology technicians
Paralegals (or legal assistants)
Physical science technicians
Research assistants
Recreation workers
Social Service aids
Teacher aides
Technical writers
(More paraprofessional opportunities will be listed in Chapter 5 under the Health Field Classification.)

TECHNICIANS

Science technicians and paraprofessionals are often closely related and electrical and electronic technicians, mechanical engineering technicians, and civil engineering technicians are at least first cousins to the paraprofessionals.

Engineering technicians can expect good opportunities in a job field that is continually growing. Employment opportunities are rising, too, for qualified technicians who are able to work with computers, communications equipment, industrial robots, and other electronic products. Similarly, there will be a steady job market for people to repair the machinery and equipment that is sold to and used by consumers. In fact, the government predicts that office machine servicers and cash register servicers will rise by 72 percent from 1982 to 1995 as offices and stores are automated.

Generally employers want to hire technicians with some post-high school training, so many technicians begin with a two-year associate degree or other specialized training.

Some of the Jobs

Aerospace technicians
Air conditioning, heating and refrigeration technicians
Broadcast technicians
Civil engineering technicians
Computer service technicians
Electrical & electronic technicians
Electrical service technicians
Food processing technicians
Instrumentation technicians
Jewelry & watch repairers
Mechanical engineering technicians
Microprocessor technicians
Motion picture projectionists
Office machine servicers
Photographic laboratory workers

Piano and organ tuners
and repairers
Robotics technicians
Solar equipment
technicians

Surveyors and surveying
technicians
Television and radio
repairers.

CLERICAL, SECRETARIAL, AND COMPUTER-RELATED JOBS

Clerical Jobs

Even though office automation will affect a great many jobs, clerical occupations are expected to remain among the most promising spots for people who do not go to college. As proof, the United States Department of Labor anticipates that employment will grow 19 to 27 percent by 1990, reaching 22.4 million or more if current trends continue. Besides the millions of jobs that will open, many more openings will be created by the need to replace the clerical workers who switch occupations or leave the labor force. In fact, replacement needs for clerical workers are projected to average more the 4 million per year between 1980 and 1990. When you start as a clerical worker, you can use your first job as a basis to move ahead in business, as evidenced by Mary Ann Pope, a branch manager and assistant vice-president of Olsten Temporary Services.

"When I got out of high school we couldn't afford college," she stated, "so I worked at a number of office jobs before I married and had children. When I returned to work at 30, I went to Olsten's for a temporary job."

As it turned out, the Olsten branch office to which Mary Ann applied needed someone to work in that office temporarily because the person who did the payroll was ill and would not be back for two months. Mary Ann was hired on the spot and when the person who was ill decided not to come back, Mary Ann was offered the job.

Job Opportunities

"I soon found out I love the temporary employment business," she declared, "so while I worked on the payroll I kept my eyes and ears open and learned what I could about interviewing and filling clients' orders."

The latter was the work Mary Ann enjoyed, and when her boss heard that he suggested she might prefer customer service and supervising the office. "That got me into the placement end of the business," she said, "so to broaden my understanding of the business I took accounting and personnel courses at night. As our branch office enlarged, my position expanded."

When the opportunity arose Mary Ann relocated and assumed the management of the Philadelphia branch. For a while she worked ten or twelve hours per day. But from her start as a payroll clerk, her efforts paid off handsomely when she was made an assistant vice president in 1981.

"My biggest advice to somebody without a degree is not to get hung up on it," she concluded. "If you need knowledge in an area and know that you don't have just go out and get it!"

Secretarial Work

Secretaries at various levels are in almost every commercial, professional, governmental, and educational office. They have come a long way from typing and shorthand, and while some people use their jobs as a stepping stone to another career, others choose to stay in this work and advance to responsible levels.

Currently, the United States Department of Labor reports that from 1980 to 1990 there is a projected growth in the number of secretarial jobs of from 28.3 percent to 37.4 percent. The demand shows no signs of slowing either, as employers state that often job vacancies remain unfilled for months before a qualified candidate can be found. Beyond that, the Bureau of Labor Statistics stresses, "Neither office automation nor economic downturns are expected to have an adverse impact on the employment of secretaries.

Automated office equipment cannot substitute for the personal qualities essential to the secretary's job." Secretaries, however, will increasingly use advanced office equipment and, as office automation becomes an integrated part of their jobs, it will free them from many routine tasks.

Depending on their background and training, secretaries can seek employment as an "all-purpose" secretary or pursue a specialized career in such fields as medicine and law. As you progress—if you are interested in being at the top of the secretarial profession—you may want to take the Certified Professional Secretary Examination given by Professional Secretaries International, 2240 Pershing Road, Crown Center, G10, Kansas City, MO 64108. You can write to the organization for information.

Computer-Related Jobs.

Most industry forecasts indicate there will be more than 10 times as many computers in use during the next decade than exist today. It is believed that by 1986 (about 100 years after the adoption of the typewriter) there will be one computer or word processing terminal for every three white collar workers. Word processing specialists will be the hub of information activities in a network of desktop terminals, computerized files, and electronic mail.

"An increasing number of workers will use computers in their jobs," believes researcher Russell Rumberger, "so my advice is that people have exposure to using computers."

"Computer skills are necessary for all workers today, and people who neglect to learn them will lose their competitive edge in the marketplace," maintains Stephen S. Roberts, a computer expert at The Catholic University of America and coauthor of the book *You Don't Have to Be a Genius to Land a Computer Job.* "There will be hundreds of thousands of openings in the coming years that will be filled by ordinary people of almost any age and background who are not science or mathematical geniuses or even college graduates."

Job Opportunities

If the computer field interests you, entry level jobs in computer operations are open to any bright high school graduate (with special computer training). For jobs that go beyond keypunch or console operator (and even for some of them) you will need special training in programming, data and word processing, and computer operations at a trade, technical, business school, or junior or community college.

Some of the Clerical, Secretarial, and Computer-Related Jobs

Accountants
Accounting clerks
Administrative assistants
Administrative secretaries
Assistant personnel clerks
Auditors
Auxilliary equipment operators
Bookkeepers
Computer console operators
Computer programmers
Court clerks
Court reporters
Data base administrators
Data processing operators
Data processing supervisors
Data typists
Executive secretaries
File clerks
Key punch operators
Legal secretaries
Medical secretaries
Micrographic specialists
Office machine operators
Payroll clerks
Printer specialists
Purchasing assistants
Receptionists
Secretaries
Shorthand reporters
Statistical clerks
Stenographers
Tape/disk librarians
Telecommunications specialists
Typists
Word processing operators
Word processing supervisors

chapter five

Service Jobs, the Government, Business, Health Care, and Sales

Long before the popular "Where's the Beef?" became a national slogan, Emilie Taylor used "Know Your Beef" to launch a career as a meat specialist, the option that was right for her.

At a very young age, Emilie started cutting meat in her father's butcher shop. Later, after her father died, she managed the family business and did every necessary task: going to the market, butchering meat, and delivering the orders. Eventually the shop was sold and Emilie reached a low in her life because butchering was all that she knew. "I tried a good many jobs after that," she said, "but wherever I went I'd talk about meat since that was what interested me."

Emilie was also a people-watcher in the stores where she bought her meat, and as she saw the meat-buying mistakes so many customers made, she decided she would have something to offer if she taught other people what she knew about meat. To get started, she packaged a "Know Your Beef" seminar and, with a strong sales approach, convinced groups and organizations to sponsor it as a program. As a result of the seminars, people began to ask her to give private classes on meat. Now, along with her programs, she runs Emilie Taylor's Meat School, a service business in which she shows students how to bone and cut various meats and turn them into specialty cuts.

SERVICE JOBS

Between 1980 and 1990 employment of service workers is expected to increase by about 24 to 32 percent, from 14.6 million to between 18.1 and 19.2 million workers.

To cite one field, the rapidly growing food-service industry is the number 1 retail employer in the United States, and the trend toward eating out is expected to add 1.8 million jobs in eating and drinking places, an increase of 38 percent from 1982 to 1995. The National Institute for the Foodservice Industry says that there are currently 85,000 openings each year for chefs and cooks in restaurants and other institutions. Thousands more start their own catering services each year.

"Hotels are another good example of where high school graduates can go through a relatively rapid career development track," says Ronald C. Pilenzo of the American Society for Personnel Administration. "Since people who come in at the bottom don't stay very long competition thins out in a hurry and you have an opportunity to prove what you can do."

Employment in transportation and driving occupations is also expected to increase somewhat because of the interest in tourism. To meet the needs of people "on-the-go," there will be job opportunities with airline, steamship, bus, and sightseeing companies. Some occupations, such as bus driver and sailor, will grow fairly slowly. Jobs in railroad transportation industries are expected to decline.

Some of the Jobs

Airline dispatchers
Appraisers
Auctioneers
Bakers
Barbers
Bartenders
Bellhops and bell captains
Bus drivers
Butchers
Casino cashiers
Casino dealers
Caterers
Cooks and chefs
Cosmetologists
Cruise directors
Customer service representatives
Dog groomers
Flight attendants
Food preparation and service workers
Funeral directors
Hair stylists
Hostesses
Hotel clerks
Hotel housekeepers
Maitre d's
Make-up artists
Masseuses and masseurs
Merchant marine sailors
Reservation/ticket/ passenger agents
Social directors
Taxi drivers
Telephone operators
Title searchers
Truck drivers
Tour guides
Waiters and waitresses

BUSINESS

Business includes such varied fields as accounting, advertising, marketing, banking, insurance, merchandising, and retailing—to mention a few examples.

From an overall view, the retail trade industry is projected to increase substantially as our growing population requires more and more shopping centers and stores. If you wish to enter this field, you can start out with beginning jobs on the basis of a high school diploma. Sometimes, with a two-year degree, you can enter management training. Nancy Brekke, for instance, graduated from The Fashion Institute of Design & Merchandising with an associate of arts degree.

She began her career in retailing in a women's ready-to-wear shop where she was soon promoted to store manager. Luckily for Nancy the store was located in a shopping center, and the center's marketing director encouraged her to interview for a special training program being offered by a major national shopping center.

Seven months after completing that training, Nancy became marketing director for four malls. Her outstanding performance prompted the company to send her to Las Vegas to open the state's most prestigious shopping complex. There her first assignment included the implementation of a major event featuring such leading designers as Bill Blass, Bob Mackie, and Albert Nipon. After other marketing director's jobs, she went to Los Angeles to be the marketing director for a very large mall.

If you like working with figures, accounting is a profession that has doubled in size in each decade for the past forty years. Many jobs require college degrees, but there is room for people with different levels of training and you can prepare for these entry positions with two years or less of intensive training at accredited business schools.

Bank services have expanded at a great rate during recent years, and over a million bank employees work in a great variety of jobs. The industry needs people with all kinds of skills, so a high school education—plus on-the-job training and continuing education—will qualify you for entry jobs.

Eleanor Carr, who is presently assistant vice-president and manager of the Catasauqua branch of the First National Bank of Allentown, Pennsylvania wanted to be a banker from a very early age. When she graduated from high school, there were no funds for college, so she followed the advice that prevailed at the time—Girls get married and have children.

After 20 years—and three children—her interest in banking was still alive, so she took a job as a teller in suburban Philadelphia. Later the family moved to Allentown, so Eleanor took a new job as teller and sometimes thought of becoming a head teller in the future, a potential that seemed remote because there were no female head tellers and no female officers in the branch system. She was undaunted, however, and her work, studying, and positive attitude paid off when she became the first woman to be placed in the bank's management program.

"It was then that I started taking courses and setting goals for myself," Eleanor recalled. "I remember, in the beginning, sending a memo to a senior officer asking if I could take a giant step and attend a management course."

Since then, Eleanor has taken thirty courses and seminars on management and participated actively in banking associations.

On the whole, community banks (those usually found in small towns, suburbs, and rural areas) are the primary employers of non-college educated individuals. The people who work within these banks are often referred to as "general practitioners" of banking because, where bank employees in large banks tend to be very specialized, each employee in a small bank is likely to be knowledgeable in several functions.

"The banking industry has traditionally been one that educates and trains its own employees," says Shirley E. Broder, Associate Director of American Bankers Association (ABA). "The American Institute of Banking (AIB) which is the educational arm of ABA educates approximately 300,000 bank employees annually throughout the United States. AIB courses are paid for completely by the bank. In addition, ABA offers one week resident schools in all the respective disciplines within a bank. These are also paid for by the employee's bank.

"Entry level positions, defined as tellers, customer service representatives, proof department staff, and most back office operation jobs are available to high school graduates with math, organizational, and communications skill," she added.

If advertising and marketing appeal to you, market research is one way to get into the field. One type of market research, as you probably know, involves interviewing people to obtain answers to questionnaires used in studies of advertising, packaging, and marketing procedures. This type also covers coding the questionnaires, tabulating data, and analyzing the results statistically.

"This is the easiest way to break into market research without having a specific educational background for it," explained a nondegree field supervisor of a research firm.

"When I graduated from high school I started to continue my education," she went on. "But when I found I was floating I decided to drop out. Subsequently I got a job working for a shopping center developer, and while I was helping with promotions for a mall, I grew interested in market research. In fact, I grew so interested that I left my permanent job and struck out for myself as a free-lance interviewer. Since I had no training for market research I did what I've already advised and started with interviewing. To get enough work to support me I contacted every market research firm I knew."

After gaining experience as a free-lance interviewer, the next step was moving to a job as an in-house interviewer with a research firm, and, ultimately, to her promotion as a field supervisor. She also took courses in business and marketing.

The life and health insurance field, which provides employment for one million people, has opportunities for people at all educational levels. Although many work in sales, many more work in nonsales and computer-related jobs.

Some of the Jobs in Business

- Accountants
- Accounting clerks
- Appraisers
- Auditors
- Bank tellers
- Bookkeeping clerks
- Bookkeeping machine operators
- Cashiers
- Claims adjusters and representatives
- Claims administrators
- Collection workers
- Credit analysts
- Data entry clerks
- Home office underwriters
- Loan processing clerks
- Market research interviewers
- Office managers
- Proof operators
- Proof supervisors
- Securities clerks
- Service representatives
- Transit clerks

GOVERNMENT JOBS

Government jobs are available at the federal, state, county, and city (or municipality and village) level, and government employees are in offices, shipyards, laboratories, national parks, hospitals, military bases, and many other settings across the country and around the world.

Most federal jobs are civil service jobs and, generally, state, county, and municipal civil service systems are organized in the same way as the federal civil service.

It is impossible to delineate all jobs because there are so many. The Council for Career Planning, Inc. sums it up by pointing out that government work includes every sort of job that exists in private business, industry, and the professions—with a few exceptions that are special to the federal government, such as delivering the mail and patrolling borders.

Competitive permanent employment in various occupations and entry-level jobs in the federal government is attained by qualifying on a United States Office of Personnel (OPM) examination appropriate to your background. When you receive a passing score, your name can be presented to a federal agency and placed on list of eligibles for employment consideration. Nondegree applicants may qualify for professional administrative jobs if their experience has been in administrative function.

You can file for these examinations by contacting the Federal Job Information Center nearest you. It will be listed in the phone book under United States Government. For a civil service job in your state, visit your State Employment Agency or check with the State Civil Service Commission (usually located in your state capitol). Information on county or local government jobs can be obtained by calling your county administration office or your city or borough hall.

Some of the Jobs

(Note their similarities to other listings)
Adminstrators
Aircraft mechanics
Artists
Automobile mechanics
Boiler and steam plant
  operators
Bookkeepers
Border patrol agents
Bus drivers and chauffers
Building inspectors
Carpenters
Clerk typists
Concrete finishers
Correction officers
Customs patrol officers
Designers
Editors
Electrical inspectors
Electricians
Electronic equipment
  repairers
File clerks
Firefighters
Food service operators
Forklift operators
Guards
Health and regulatory
  inspectors
Hospital attendants
Law enforcement officers
Machinists
Machinery repairers
Mail carriers
Mechanical inspectors

Medical technologists
Nurses
Painters
Pipefitters
Plumbers
Police officers
Postal clerks
Postal inspectors
Printers
Programmers
Researchers
Secretaries
Sheetmetal workers
Steamfitters
Surveyors
Teachers
Telephone operators
Truck drivers
Typists
Writers

HEALTH

Continued population growth and expansion of health care insurance coverage are primary reasons underlying the continued growth in the health field. In addition, the aged, who require the most health care, are on the increase. Between 1980 and 1995 people above 65 years will increase by 26 percent.

The number of registered nurses is expected to grow by 49 percent between 1982 and 1995, providing an additional 642,000 jobs; nursing aides and orderlies will add 423,000 new jobs; and licensed practical nurses, 220,000 jobs. Among the smaller occupations, physical therapy technicians are projected to increase by 68 percent and medical assistants by 47 percent.

Educational programs for jobs in the health field can be found in institutions, ranging from the traditional hospital setting to a growing number of junior and community colleges. For many of the jobs, specialized training beyond high school is required, and programs offering alternative types of training are sponsored by vocational/technical schools, proprietary schools, United States government institutions, and other health care facilties. In some cases—dispensing opticians, for instance—there are apprenticeships.

"Many people do not realize that work as a dispensing

optician is available without a college degree and a long academic program," said a dispensing optician who opened her own business. "Each state has different rules. In New Jersey, where I trained, you can prepare for this work in two ways."

One way is a four-year apprenticeship under a licensed optician. The other is a four-year program, combining two years of optical school at a two-year college and two years of apprenticeship. Many states—but not all—require a license, and before you can get one you must pass a stringent examination given by the State Board of Opticians. (Contact your State Board for Dispensing Opticians for specific information for your state.) After you are licensed, you can work for retail optical shops, department stores, and other retail stores that sell prescription lenses. Many dispensing opticians own their own optical shops.

"I married an optician," our informant for this field said, "and like many wives I started out helping him with his bookkeeping part time. I loved every moment in the office, so I soon began to show and suggest frames that would fit people's faces and go well with their prescriptions. I also watched my husband work and before too long I learned to work on the machines myself.

"Once I decided this was the work for me, I obtained an apprentice permit from the State Board of Opticians to begin my training under my husband. I also enrolled in courses at a community college. You can learn a lot about dispensing and machinery in a shop. But technical courses and a foundation in physics and sciences give you a background you can't obtain simply by working in a shop.

"In fact, I'd go so far as to say that people considering an apprenticeship would be wise to take a few courses first to familiarize themselves with the field. Then, when they go to opticians and ask for a chance to learn, they have something to offer. I'd also advise an apprentice to seek training with an independent optician rather than a chain because in my opinion you get more experience this way."

Some of the Jobs

(For many jobs in the health field you will need certification or licensing by an accredited agency. Information on this is included in the Resource Directory.)

Cyotechnologists
Dental assistants
Dental hygienists
Dental laboratory
  technicians
Diagnostic medical
  sonographers
Dispensing opticians and
  optical technicians
Electrocardiograph
  technicians
Electrocephalographic
  technologists
Emergency medical
  technicians—paramedics
Histologic technicians
Laboratory technicians
Licensed practical nurses
Medical assistants
Medical Laboratory
  technicians
Medical record technicians
  and clerks
Nuclear medicine
  technologists
Nurses aides, orderlies and
  attendants
Occupational therapy
  assistants
Operating room
  technicians
Optometric assistants
Physical therapy assistants
Radiation therapy
  technologists
Respiratory therapists
Registered nurses
Surgical technologists
X-ray technicians

SALES

Sales occupations are expected to be one of the leaders in growth in the number of jobs through 1995. Although some jobs are salaried ones, others are on commission. The latter is where the big earnings are. Often you will find the earnings exceed what you would earn on a typical corporate job.

As things stand now, employment for securities sales workers, real estate agents, wholesale trade sales workers, and travel agents looks particularly good and is expected to grow more rapidly than the average sales job. The Bureau of Labor Statistics predicts that openings for travel agents alone will rise more than 40 percent—about 25,000 more than in 1982—in the next decade.

While a college degree is helpful in the financial sales service industry, it is not always necessary. In *Self* magazine, "Big Money Careers: M.B.A. Not Needed" by Cathryn Jakobson, Paula D. Hughes, first vice-president of Thomson McKinnon Securities stated: "When I hire personnel I'm not interested in degrees and diplomas. I want someone who's eager to learn, who really cares. Those are the critical qualities—and they don't come with a certificate."

Security brokers (also known as registered representatives or account executives) buy and sell stocks, bonds, mutual funds, and other financial products. If you are interested in this field you would do well to have sales experience behind you as potential employers will want to see whether you will be able to service the financial needs of others.

In her article, Cathryn Jakobson points out that if you cannot get into a broker training program in a brokerage house or other financial institution, you might consider entering the field as a secretary or sales assistant and then climbing to the account executive (or registered rep) rung through that entry level job. To become a registered rep you must first be sponsored by a firm belonging to the National Association of Securities Dealers (NASD) and then pass an NASD-administered licensing exam.

For real estate, you will need to supplement your high school diploma with an approved real estate course and then take a state licensing exam. In insurance, most companies will accept people with high school diplomas and work experience for jobs as life and health insurance agents. On-the-job training is provided, and business-sponsored education programs are available. Agents must be licensed in the state in which they sell life and health insurance. To obtain this license, they must usually pass an examination given by their state insurance department.

For some sales jobs you will not need specific post-high school education. In one instance, a woman who eventually worked up to a spot as director of sales for a large hotel simply "showed up" for a hotel job interview. After graduating from high school she began selling immediately. A personnel agency subsequently sent her to a Chicago hotel chain, and her career in hospitality began when she was hired for a job there.

"I worked as a secretary in the catering department for about a year and a half, booking catering affairs, assisting sales people in finalizing their programs, and gaining a knowledge of kitchen and food production," she reported. "Later I became sales secretary to the sports representative."

After gaining experience on that job, she was promoted to director of sales for one of the chain's hotels in the east. As director, she was also sports representative, so part of her responsibility was seeing that sports teams could enjoy their privacy and have all their needs filled while they were at the hotel. The other part of her job involved handling group sales, servicing groups so they would rebook, and meeting budgeted dollars and profit goals.

"If you're interested in this type of sales, get as much selling experience as you can," she advised. "Business education and business sense are very important too."

Some of the Jobs

Automobile dealers and salespeople
Direct selling personnel
Hotel sales personnel
Life and Health insurance agents
Manufacturers salespeople
Real estate agents
Retail trade salespeople
Sales assistants
Sales clerks
Securities brokers
Whole sale trade salespeople
Travel agents

MAIL ORDER, FRANCHISING, AND CONSULTING

An exploration of the sales field would not be complete without the inclusion of these "best-selling" opportunities: mail order, franchising, and consulting.

No one can talk about mail order without thinking of Lillian Vernon, an enterprising self-made millionaire and "Dear Lillian" to millions of people who receive her mail order catalogues each year. In her more than thirty years in the mail order catalog business, she has seen mail order change from a game of chance operated from basements and kitchen tables to the kind of entrepreneurship that calls for top professionalism.

Success stories such as hers make thousands of men and women consider selling by mail. However, the mortality rate in mail order is high, so investigate it thoroughly before you make a move. Read books on the subject and study the mail order sections of magazines. Send for catalogs. Notice prices, headlines, copy, type faces, and photography. Order items from different firms and analyze the services and products. Finally, when you are ready to launch your business, choose a trendy and timely product of your own or an item you buy from a wholesale gift market. The Gift and Art Center, 225 Fifth Ave., New York, NY 10010 is a source for the latter.

Franchising

Some people choose to be their own bosses through a franchise operation. In a franchise, a parent company grants an individual (or group) the right to market its products or services in a specified territory. There are approximately 1,500 franchise companies, representing 40 different industries in the United States, and the International Franchise Association (IFA), an organization that sets standards of businesss practice and serves as a central point for franchise data, reports that one out of every three retail sales dollars comes from a franchise business.

Like any business venture, franchises entail risks and challenges—and many fail. But some business analysts say that a person managing a franchise has a greater chance of succeeding than entrepreneurs starting other businesses. Andrew Kostecka, a Commerce Department analyst states: "Franchising is one of the safest ways to get people into business." Martin Boehm, research analyst at IFA adds: "Since small businesses often fail because of lack of experience and expertise, the advantage of a franchise is the track record of the company."

When considering a franchise, your first step is selecting a reliable company that has a good record and history. This is extremely important because franchising, along with other industries, has its fly-by-night, get-rich-quick firms.

Even if you are confident that your franchiser is up to snuff, be cautious. "We recommend that people look at a purchase document, speak to other franchises in a chain, and talk to their attorney and accountant," says Martin Boehm. "For those with cash, franchising can be a way to buy a job. But it's not without its problems. It's for someone who can take charge of a situation but still follow a game plan. It can't be somebody who's totally innovative. Since the franchisee is not allowed to tamper a whole lot with a product, that person might become totally frustrated.

The IFA publishes a *Classified Directory of Members* that lists the names and addresses of companies that have been accepted into membership after meeting stringent requirements and subscribing to a business Code of Ethics. You can request it from International Franchise Association, 1025 Connecticut Ave., NW, Washington, DC 20036. The IFA also publishes *Investigate Before Investing*, which provides guidance for prospective franchisees. These publications are available for a small price.

Consulting

"It doesn't take a wall full of degrees to be a successful consultant," explains Howard Shenson, the consultant's consultant. "Thousands of people with marketable skills—but no college degree—are discovering consulting. What you *do* need is a feel for marketing your knowledge and a great belief in yourself. As an expert, you must offer advice not only about problems, but, also, about how to solve them."

Granted, when you hear the word "consultant" you generally think of M.B.A.s who sell management, financial, or marketing expertise. However, while many consultants work in that area, others peddle their expertise in a completely different way.

"There are consultants who advise consumers on how to wire a home for a video or stereo system," commented Shenson, who publishes *The Professional Consultant* newsletter, 20121 Ventura Boulevard, Woodland Hills, CA 91364. "One of my students—the manager of a small FM radio station—went into the radio consulting business and now he advises producers and managers about programming and appealing to various audiences."

Other examples of Shenson's students include:

- A widow in Texas who had never held a job in her life, but who was always told she threw good parties. She is now a party consultant who advises both corporate and private clients on how to give successful parties.
- A retired California stamp collector who is now a stamp-collecting consultant, advising investors who wish to put their money into valuable collections.
- An Illinois couple that worked as a butler and maid, and then discovered there was more money to be made as consultants advising people how to select and train domestic help.
- A Michigan man with a reputation for driving a hard bargain when buying a car, who became a consultant to people buying cars.
- An 18-year-old boy in California who was a good skateboarder, and who now earns his living as a skateboard consultant, advising businessmen how to design and build skateboard parks.

"That young boy knew the skateboard business," said Shenson, "and—I repeat—if you know your stuff you don't need a string of degrees. I have run into scores of people who have been successful in consulting even though they did not have a formal education. They applied their know-how and 'street smarts.'"

Like any other business, there are also failures in consulting. However, if people are always asking you questions and seeking you out for your knowledge of a particular subject, you might think of this alternative. The pay is usually high and, as an example of how people can make more money consulting than by actually practicing their skills, Shenson continued talking about the butler and maid.

"When they were actually *being* a butler and a maid, their income was limited to whatever the one family who was using them was able to pay them," he said. "But by becoming consultants, they could line up 50 clients who needed consulting in that area and charge each a very nice sum."

READ ALL ABOUT IT!

As mentioned in previous chapters, whenever a job field appeals to you, refer to the Resource Directory. Then write to the organizations that represent that field. For addresses of other organizations that cover career fields, consult the Encyclopedia of Associations found in most public libraries.

Additional publications to check in libraries are the Occupational Outlook Handbook, the Dictionary of Occupational Titles, Occupational Projections and Training Data, and the Encyclopedia of Careers and Vocational Guidance. State employment offices often have free booklets about jobs and careers, and the Government Printing Office has bulletins. For the latter, write to the Superintendent of Documents, United States Government Printing Office, Washington, DC 20402 for a current listing. Many pamphlets are free.

Finally look for job and career workshops, courses, seminars, and gatherings that bring diverse people together to talk about their work. Generally you can find these programs listed in daily newspapers. Investigate each until you find the one that will serve your needs the best. Also, before you pay any fees, talk to program directors and check the credentials of the people who will be running the programs. Whenever you can, learn the names of people who have used a service or taken a course and ask what help they received.

chapter six

What the Armed Forces Can Offer You

Prior to joining the Air Force in the hope of becoming a physician's assistant, Kathleen Ross (not her real name) had been a hospital records clerk. However, medical experience was required for entrance into the physician's assistant program, so Kathleen was told that she would have to start in another field.

As an alternative, she entered under a general enlistment option, which meant that during basic training she would be offered a choice of occupation. Fortunately, when the time came, work as a medical services assistant (comparable to a licensed practical nurse) was one of the choices.

Once Kathleen made her choice, her medical training began with a bus ride to Sheppard Air Force Base for a six-week program. Following her training Kathleen had to pass an examination. After proving herself as a medical services assistant, she could progress in the medical field through additional training.

The foregoing story, related by Neal Baxter in the United States Department of Labor's *Occupational Outlook Quarterly*, points up another alternative to four years of college. When you choose the Armed Forces, your training and subsequent job experience will be as up-to-date as tomorrow.

Because the service is a world of its own, it needs many of the same kinds of workers found in civilian life, and except in the case of officers, a college degree is not usually required. In the Army, for instance, less than 10 percent of the enlisted force have four-year degrees. Some of the civilian occupations with military counterparts are shown in Figure 6-1.

In one case a midwesterner who enlisted in the Army started as a mechanic. As he advanced and took courses, he learned a great deal about radar and sophisticated electronics. After his Army days, he decided to use his training for a research job in high-level electronics.

In order to get help in reaching this goal, he went to the John C. Crystal Center. After going through the course, he returned to the midwest and approached a large radio

FIGURE 6-1

Some Civilian Occupations With Military Counterparts.

Accounting clerk
Airplane flight attendant
Air traffic control specialist
Announcer
Asphalt-paving machine operator
Audio-video repairer
Automobile body repairer
Automobile mechanic
Automobile upholsterer
Baker
Barber
Blood-bank technologist
Bookkeeper
Bricklayer
Bulldozer operator
Butcher
Cable splicer
Camera operator, television
Cargo agent
Carpenter
Cashier
Cement mason
Central office operator
Central office repairer
Chemical laboratory technician
Clerk typist
Computer operator
Computer peripheral equipment operator
Concrete-paving machine operator
Construction equipment mechanic
Construction worker
Cook
Dental assistant
Dental hygienist
Dental laboratory technician
Diesel mechanic
Diver
Drafter
Electrical instrument repairer
Electrician
Electric motor repairer
Electrocardiograph technician
Electroencephalograph technologist
Embalmer
Firefighter
Flight engineer
Guard
Illustrator
Industrial engineering technician
Inspector, boiler
Instrument mechanic
Laboratory technician
Legal secretary
Locksmith
Machinist
Maintenance machinist
Medical records clerk
Medical service technician
Medical technologist
Metallurgical technician
Molder
Motion picture projectionist
Musician
Nurse aid
Occupational therapy aid
Offset press operator
Optician, dispensing
Painter
Patternmaker
Payroll clerk
Personnel clerk
Pharmacist's assistant
Photographer
Physical therapists's assistant
Plumber
Police officer
Post office clerk
Precision lens grinder
Press operator
Procurement clerk
Prosthetics technician
Psychiatric aid
Radiologic technologist
Radio mechanic
Refrigeration mechanic
Respiratory therapist
Rigger
Sheet metal worker
Shipping clerk
Shorthand reporter
Sound mixer
Sound technician
Sous chef
Stationary engineer
Statistical clerk
Stenographer
Stock clerk
Surgical technician
Television and radio repairer
Travel clerk
Truckdriver
Veterinary hospital attendant
Watch repairer
Water treatment plant operator
Welder

Source: Occupational Outlook Quarterley/Fall 1983

FIGURE 6-2

Apprenticeships in the following occupations are offered in the military. All are available in the Army unless otherwise indicated.

- Air-Traffic communication technician (Marine Corps only)
- Air-Traffic control radar technician
- Air-Traffic control technician (Marine Corps only)
- Air-Traffic navigational aids technician (Marine Corps only)
- Aircraft electrical mechanic
- Aircraft engine mechanic (turbine)
- Aircraft mechanic, armament
- Airplane mechanic
- Artillery repairer
- Construction equipment mechanic (Marine Corps only)
- Cook (Marine Corps and Navy)
- Drafter (architectural)
- Electrical instrument repairer
- Electrical mechanic (aircraft)
- Electrical repairer (Marine Corps also)
- Electrician (Marine Corps and Navy)
- Electrician, radio
- Electro-mechanical technician
- Fire control instrument repairer
- Fire control system repairer
- Firefighter
- Fuel systems repairer
- Grading and paving equipment operator
- Heavy-duty equipment mechanic
- Heavy-duty repairer (construction equipment)
- Helicopter mechanic
- Hydraulic equipment mechanic
- Illustrator
- Industrial electrician/repairer
- Marine heavy-duty mechanic (heavy-duty mechanic—diesel)
- Marine hull repairer, ironworker (boatbuilder—steel)
- Meteorologist (Navy only)
- Molder (Navy only)
- Office machine servicer (Navy also)
- Off-set press operator (Marine Corps only)
- Ordnance artificer
- Photograph interpreter
- Photographer, motion
- Radio communications technician
- Radio mechanic (Marine Corps also)
- Radio operator
- Radio/television repairer
- Refrigeration/air-conditioning repairer/servicer
- Refrigeration mechanic (Marine Corps only)
- Rigger
- Sewing machine repairer
- Sheet metal worker (aircraft)

Automatic equipment technician
Automobile body repairer and painter
Automobile mechanic (Marine Corps only)
Automotive electrical systems repairer
Baker (Marine Corps only)
Cable splicer
Camera repairer (Navy only)
Carpenter (Marine Corps only)
Central office telephone installer and repairer (Marine Corps only)
Electronic mechanic (Marine Corps also)
Electronic mechanic (radar)
Electronic technician
Electronic technician (communications)
Electronic technician (radar)
Electronic technician (radio/TV)
Electronic warfare intercept systems repairer
Field engineer (microwave)
Industrial welder
Instrument repairer (electronic)
Laboratory technician (petroleum)
Land surveyor (Marine Corps only)
Line installer/repairer
Lithographer (offset press operator)
Lithographer platemaker (Navy also)
Machinist (Navy only)
Maintenance mechanic (Navy only)
Maintenance mechanic, hydraulic equipment (aircraft) picture
Photographer, still (Navy also)
Photographic equipment maintenance technician
Plant equipment operator
Plumber (Marine Corps only)
Plumber, pipefitter
Powerhouse electrician/repairer
Production coordinator (radio/TV broadcasting)
Pumper-gauger (petro-chemical)
Small weapons repairer
Station installer/repairer (wire systems)
Stationary engineer (Navy only)
Surveyor (artillery)
Surveyor, engineering
Telegraphic-teletypewriter operator
Television cable installer
Truck mechanic
Universal equipment operator (construction equipment)
Welder, combination (Marine Corps only)

Source: Occupational Outlook Quarterly/Fall 1983

company. He devised a forceful sales approach and—without a college degree—landed a job as assistant to the director of scientific research.

"The director couldn't care less whether he had college," Crystal stated. "He had the skills and background that the director needed."

DECIDING IF THE SERVICE IS FOR YOU

Before considering the service you need to make sure it is the right decision for you as it requires a long-term commitment to serving and defending the country, and a willingness to take and follow orders. As Neal Baxter stated in his article: "Bear in mind that the Armed Services are not for everyone—nor is Harvard, for that matter." Consequently, before you decide on the service, consider what you expect from it and what it will expect from you.

If you decide that it is for you, the skills you learn in your technical and vocational instruction will depend on several things: your ability to qualify based on tests; your choice; and the availability of skill training at the time. Often the training programs for some of the very popular occupations are difficult to get into, and, in many cases, the qualified are chosen for them on a first-come-first-served basis. Most branches of the services have a Delayed Entry Program that is designed to help high school students plan their futures by allowing them to enlist during their senior year and then delay entry until after graduation.

ADDITIONAL TRAINING OPPORTUNITIES

To help you advance and develop skills, you can take courses in your off-duty time. The service will pay a large percentage of the cost for approved courses and, in some instances, you can supplement other training with two-year community college programs or home-study courses.

A New Englander who spent three years in the Coast Guard completed seventeen home-study courses given by the United States Coast Guard Institute. He did so well that he rose to Second Class Petty Officer and then to First Class. Moreover, the various skills he learned while studying and serving on a Coast Guard cutter enabled him to initiate a program to increase the ship's accuracy in positioning buoys and channel markers using a programmable calculator. Now, in his civilian life, the program he initiated in the service benefits both commercial vessels and pleasure craft in New England waters.

Most branches of the service, with the cooperation of the Department of Labor, also offer an Apprenticeship Program. Basically, this program lets you build a log of written documented evidence that shows that you have worked in a specific skill and that you have experience that can be applied to a similar civilian position. Just by working at a skill and logging your hours, you get closer to a journeyman's status every day. When you meet all the requirements, you receive a Certificate of Completion of Apprenticeship from the Department of Labor. Figure 6-2 shows some of the apprenticeships that are offered. All are available in the Army unless otherwise indicated.

WHERE TO GET MORE INFORMATION

Enlistment programs vary, but all applicants for the five branches must meet age, citizenship, moral, physical, and educational standards and pass certain tests. For specifics for each branch, and detailed information on educational and occupational opportunities (and for pay and allowances), check with local recruiters. To locate the recruiter in your area, ask at your local post office or consult the Yellow Pages under "Recruiting."

III

HOW TO GET THE SKILLS YOU NEED AND MARKET THE SKILLS YOU HAVE

chapter seven

Dozens of New Alternatives to College Education

When Joseph Nicolato, the senior vice-president of Volvo of America Corporation, returned from military service he took the best job he could find—a warehouseman's job for Volvo. He enrolled in college courses at night. He did not continue for his degree because he had other priorities and despised sitting in classrooms.

One of his main priorities was advancing in his job so, after thirteen months, when there was a stock control and purchasing job open he suggested that he could bring a plus to that job because he knew the warehouse operational work.

"After thirteen months in the purchasing job I suggested establishing a parts order office to serve as a central location for calls from dealers because I'd observed how confusing it was to have dealers call up at random to place orders over the phone," he explained.

When Nicolato made that suggestion, he was given the opportunity to organize and develop a parts order office. "While I was in the parts order office I began to see that instead of trying to train dealers over the phone, someone from the company ought to be out in the field training them in their dealerships," he said. "Approaching my boss on that resulted in my spending a year covering 25 states and 250 dealers as the first parts representative for Volvo in North America."

Following Nicolato's year on the road, he was called into his boss's office and offered a job in which he would be involved in assisting the parts manager. Unfortunately, he was told at that time that he could not be given the title of "assistant parts manager."

"Here's where you can run into a no-college-degree situation," Nicolato pointed out. "Sometimes when you reach a certain point, a company may resist letting you go further because you lack the degree. I had those college courses from my earlier start, and I'd been taking specialized automotive business courses. But since I didn't have the degree I had to make the decision of whether to say, 'I won't take the job if I don't get the title' or whether to try to work it out in some other way. As an investment in my career I said, "I'll take the position and prove to you guys that I deserve to be assistant parts manager.'"

In a year Nicolato was given the title. Four years later, he was made parts manager. Subsequently he progressed to zone manager, assistant to the president, and then a vice-president. In 1976 he was put in charge of the eastern half of the country, prior to becoming senior vice-president for North American operations.

"There *are* alternatives to college," he declared. "Vocational education is one. A company that has a program where you can get work-related education is another. Community college courses at night are advantageous too because the words 'some college' look good on resumes and are probably enough to get you an interview. It's also always impressive to say 'I plan to go to school in the evenings.'"

Whatever your plans for the future are, you will do well to add to your general education some specialized, hands-on practical training. As Nicolato indicated, this training is available at vocational-technical institutes; community (or junior) colleges; and from company-sponsored programs. Other alternatives are: adult school and continuing education courses; work-study programs; correspondence schools; internships; apprenticeships; career schools; self-education; on-the-job experience; and working and learning at the same time.

When you decide against college, this need for alternatives is imperative as observers of the job scene stress that four out of five of the jobs on the market require post-high school training. In the American Vocational Association's *Voc Ed Journal,* Christopher Davis offers the following insight: "There's a serious problem in today's job market that is leaving millions of Americans high, dry, and jobless. In essence, we have a job market in this nation that screams out with opportunity, promises great hope and prosperity for tomorrow, yet goes begging for qualified applicants to fill jobs. Why? Because there is one major prerequisite in today's job market: skills. Skills are the job insurance of the future."

"So are ideas and learning by doing," points out Suzanne Hill, head of Hill Management Corporation and an entertainment consultant for several large hotel chains. "If you're a resourceful 'idea' person who listens, reads, gets involved with people, and goes through life with your eyes wide open, life can be your teacher. When I have an idea that stimulates my mind I want the chance to try it and see whether it will work.

"I didn't want college," Suzanne continued, "but I had some training and experience in singing so, after high school, I took the first alternative that came along and began singing at New York's former Biltmore Hotel when a British band leader started an orchestra."

Later, after marriage and children, Suzanne participated in the ownership-management of a golf club with her husband. During that time she made good contacts with the celebrities and advertising people who were members, and one day one of them suggested she try making television commercials. She took the challenge and was off and running with her first visit to an advertising agency.

Once Suzanne returned to work, one thing led to another and she ultimately wound up booking entertainment, which got her into being an entertainment consultant to several hotel chains. While doing this, she was offered the opportunity to direct a large recreational facility. Here, along with producing entertainment, she supervised the swimming pool, health spa, sports, adult education classes, meeting and conference rooms, payroll and a staff of fifty people.

When I took the job I had no experience in this kind of work," she acknowledged. "But I learned by osmosis and doing and, after three and one half years, launched my own leisure management corporation to provide complete service for swimming pools in elegant hi-rises on the Hudson River. I really think we can learn anything we want to if we have an open attitude, so I'd say to any non-degree person 'Do things you want to do and say Yes as the opportunities come.'"

Training and experience are the tickets to opportunities. The following alternatives and options offer the chance to obtain training and experience.

COMMUNITY AND JUNIOR COLLEGES

By providing a wide variety of day and evening programs, community and junior colleges enable many students from diverse backgrounds to obtain occupational and educational training. The training you get can be substantial, too, because in 1984 a Group Attitudes Corporation survey showed that Americans are quite satisfied with the high quality of instruction at community and junior colleges and tend to feel that such two-year institutions provide a sound education at a low or reasonable cost. Of those polled, 75.9 percent felt that an associate's degree from a two-year college was very useful in helping a person obtain a job.

For example, Michael Grant Martin graduated from a two-year institution with an associate's degree in interior design. One year after graduation he was employed as the only space planner for Prudential Life Insurance Company's western region. He was selected from 125 candidates and he supervised space planning for both large and small facilities. Working from a blueprint, he designed raw space or redesigned existing space to reflect the interior design needs of completed facilities.

At community and junior colleges, you will find hundreds of courses to choose from on topics as diverse as creative arts, management development, construction technology, and computer applications. Some programs last less than two years and grant certificates. There are also workshops, seminars, and short-term courses.

WORKING AND LEARNING AT THE SAME TIME

The ultimate in training is to work and learn at the same time—either by working and going to school on the side or by going to school and working on the side. Many alternatives to the four-year degree allow you to fit your courses around working full or part time, and there are definite advantages to planning your training this way. For example, you will learn the valuable lesson of how to do two things at once.

One outstandingly successful nondegree person who enthusiastically subscribes to the theory of always having something on the side is Allen E. Paulson, the chairman of the board and president and chief executive officer of Gulfstream Aerospace Corporation.

For Paulson, doing two things at once began when his parents separated. At 13, he had to support himself by selling newspapers and cleaning the lobby and bathrooms in an old family hotel. When he was 15, he and two other people split a prize of $100 playing bingo at the movies. Paulson used his $33.33 share to buy a $30.17 bus ticket to California where he got a job on a dairy farm. Milking cows was one on-the-side job he held while he went to high school. Through other jobs he learned to repair cars and farm equipment, and fell in love with airplanes.

After graduating from high school, Paulson moved to West Virginia for a job with the du Pont Corporation. On the side he worked part time in construction and entered the University of West Virginia to study electrical engineering. He dropped out of college when he saw an advertisement for a mechanic for Trans World Airlines. The job soon showed him that aviation was the field for him, so during World War II he entered the Army Air Corps, attended flight and ground school, and gained some flying experience. Following his discharge, he continued in aviation, financing the completion of his pilot training partially through the G. I. Bill and partially by starting an automobile repair garage—on the side, of course. He also returned to TWA.

While he was working as a mechanic, the Federal Aeronautics Administration adopted a regulation requiring a flight engineer in the cabin on all passenger flights. Because TWA did not have enough flight engineers to meet the requirements, it turned some of its mechanics into flight engineers. Paulson was one. His next step, while continuing to work full time for TWA, was to expand his garage by buying old cars, repairing them, and reselling them at a profit. Later he expanded further by applying the same methods to refurbishing old airplanes.

That was the beginning of Paulson's rise, and in 1951 he founded his own company to specialize in converting surplus airline passenger aircraft to cargo configurations. Between 1951 and 1981 he bought and founded several other aircraft companies, bought a Lear jet distributorship, and, in 1982, founded Gulfstream Aerospace Corporation.

"Learn everything you can every step of the way" is his ongoing credo.

PRIVATE CAREER/VOCATIONAL/TECHNICAL SCHOOLS

Known as proprietary institutions, these "no frills" schools operate at a profit and offer career development programs that lead to diplomas, and, for some courses, to two-year associate's degrees. Tuition fees can range from $1000 to $4000 with an average of $2500 for a 10-month course. Large schools typically offer a variety of programs in several vocational areas. Some business schools, for example, offer shorthand, typing, stenography, and many offer fundamentals of accounting and computer operations. Many trade schools offer courses ranging from air-conditioning installation and repair to welding and cutting operations. Small schools specialize in one program, such as cosmetology or radiologic technology. For specific information on a variety of schools, consult *Lovejoy's Career and Vocational School Guide* in your library.

"Technical schools may not carry as much weight as college in the minds of scholars," says photographer Jean Deer. "But they teach you the specifics in a short time and then you can use the training and act upon what you've gained."

Another person who proves you can do this is Joann Catafamo, who graduated from a Washington business school in a legal secretarial program. After her graduation she was employed by a law firm. When one of the firm's attorneys was appointed to a position with the Federal Department of Justice, Joann left the firm to work for him. During her years in his office she was responsible for supervising fifteen secretaries, and she had contact with the White House on a regular basis.

HOW TO SELECT THE RIGHT PROPRIETARY SCHOOL

The Association of Independent Colleges and Schools (AICS), the National Home Study Council (NHSC), the Cosmetology Accrediting Commission, and the National Association of Trade and Technical Schools (NATTS) all sponsor independent accreditation commissions that maintain educational standards and business ethics. For a listing of over 700 accredited trade and technical schools and a description of 98 careers, write for a free *Handbook of Trade and Technical Careers and Training* to NATTS, 2251 Wisconsin Avenue, NW, Suite 200, Washington, DC 20007. You can also obtain information from AICS, One Dupont Circle, NW, Suite 350, Washington DC 20036. In addition, you can get names and addresses of schools by writing to your State Department of Education in the state capitol, as each state Approval and Licensing Agency publishes a "Directory of Approved Private Trade and Technical Schools."

When a school is accredited, it has passed a thorough examination of its educational quality, teaching ability, and administrative integrity by an accrediting agency recognized by the United States Department of Education. Look for this mark of accreditation when you are selecting a school. To be sure that you choose a reputable school,

NATTS advises asking for catalogs at three or more schools. Then, before you enroll, get the answers to the following questions.

1. Are the courses up-to-date? How long will training take and will you be trained for jobs that exist?
2. Does the school have a laboratory or shop that provides hands-on training and duplicates a real work environment?
3. Does the school help find jobs for graduates and at what types of jobs are the graduates placed? Ethically and legally schools cannot guarantee employment, but most have placement offices that try to match graduates with jobs. What proportion of students find employment upon completion of this training?
4. What kind of buildings, classrooms, facilities, and equipment does the school offer? Is the equipment current?
5. What is the total cost of tuition, supplies, and fees? Can you realistically afford the school? What is the school's refund policy?
6. Is the school licensed by the state post secondary school licensing bureau? This should be in the catalog.

In addition, visit the school, preferably when classes are in session, and discuss the courses and your expectations with administrators and teachers. If possible, speak to students and graduates. Also phone prospective employers in the area and ask if their companies use the same kind of equipment that the school uses and if they hire graduates. Sometimes it is a good idea to contact the Better Business Bureau in your area and inquire about schools.

In their book *Getting Skilled*, Tom Hebert and John Coyne stress reading all contracts or other binding agreements carefully before signing. Be sure that the school's schedule of payments, tuition refund policy, and clauses covering cancellation are clearly spelled out.

APPRENTICESHIPS

In an article on apprenticeships in *On Your Own* magazine, Tevere MacFadyen tells the story of 20-year-old Mike Mefferd, an apprentice at a Maine institution called the Apprenticeshop. Along with 14 other apprentices ranging in age from 20 to 48 (and at least one has a college degree), Mefferd enrolled at the Apprenticeshop for a two-year term to study and practice the art of wooden boat building. He is learning his trade by working under the watchful eyes of a master builder and assistant, by exchanging ideas with other apprentices, and, above all, by doing.

Early in his senior year in high school, Mefferd knew he did not want to go to college. He was interested in working with his hands, so he wrote to cabinetmaker shops, vocational-technical institutes, and schools that teach students to make musical instruments. One of his letters went to a boatbuilder, who wrote back to suggest the Apprenticeshop.

The founder and director of this unique apprenticeship program is Lance Lee, the son of a boatbuilder and himself a graduate of Bowdoin College. "One part of me believes in a college education," he said in *On Your Own*. "It can be a terrific discipline. Boatbuilding, though, is pretty nearly perfect as a center of study. To build a boat you've got to use forethought. You have to learn how to think things through and plan ahead. It makes people thoughtful and careful in a way that no college course I've ever heard of can."

Generally apprenticeships for boatbuilding and other jobs that require high technical manual skills involve a combination of on-the-job training and related classroom instruction—usually 144 to 200 hours each year. The classroom instruction teaches apprentices the theoretical as well as practical aspects of the job at trade, technical, vocational, or correspondence schools.

For on-the-job training, apprentices work on jobs under the supervision of certified journeyworkers. Most apprenticeship programs last from three to five years, and when you enter a program you make a formal written agreement with an employer stating how much you will earn, how long you will be in training, and what you will be taught. Generally there is a probationary period of six months during which the employer may end the program. After that the employer must allow you to finish the program if you want to and there is work for you to do. By the same token, you are free to leave the program at any time.

Apprentices usually (but not always) start earning forty to fifty percent of the journeyworker's wage for their trade and receive increases every six months if progress is satisfactory. Apprentices nearing the end of their programs are generally earning ninety to ninety-five percent of the journeyworker's wage. Sometimes apprentices also receive fringe benefits and free tools.

National apprenticeship standards approved by the Bureau of Apprenticeship and Training or State Apprenticeship Councils govern the scope of work, courses of instruction, length of training, and amount of pay. Apprentices who complete an apprenticeship program are given certificates that show they are fully qualified as highly skilled journeyworkers or skilled craft workers. Often the upper age limit for many programs is twenty-five.

Apprenticeship programs are not always easy to get into for either men or women and, if you look for an apprenticeship in an area in which sixty percent of the journeymen are unemployed you are likely to face a problem. Qualifications vary from program to program, but almost all require a high school diploma or General Educational Development (GED) certificate. You can learn more about apprenticeships and how to qualify and apply for them by writing to the Bureau of Apprenticeship and Training, U.S. Department of Labor, 601 D Street, NW, Room 6100, Washington, DC 20213. Another source is the Apprenticeship Information Centers, operated by state employment services. Still a third is the Occupational Outlook Handbook in your library.

Most apprenticeship programs have committees of

employers and local trade unions that interview applicants, review the trainee's progress, and determine when an apprenticeship has been completed satisfactorily. This brings us to the subject of unions, as one of the largest and perhaps the most familiar union training program is the apprenticeship.

UNIONS

Although several economic and social trends are threatening the status of unions and putting them into positions where they are not flourishing as in the past, more than 100 national and international unions are affiliated with the American Federation of Labor and Congress of Industrial Organizations (AFL-CIO). Along with steel workers, auto workers, rubber workers, and construction workers; teachers, firefighters, government employees, technicians, newspaper reporters, actors, entertainers, barbers, hairdressers, machinists, bus drivers, railroad workers, telephone operators, television cameramen, and printers have formed their own special unions, just to mention a few examples. All subscribe to the viewpoint that the emphasis on education as the surest means of ensuring job security, promotional capability, and work-life opportunities must now receive more intensive attention than at any other time in our history.

Regardless of the changes in store for unions, their attention to comprehensive training seems destined to remain on the upswing. For instance, the United Brotherhood of Carpenters and Joiners of America is putting forth an all-out effort not only to train as many people as possible for entry into the field of carpentry, but to offer training in upgrading skills to those who are already journeymen carpenters.

Speaking for another union, Dr. Lionel Bruce Kingery, International Representative, Education Department of the United Automobile, Aerospace & Agricultural Implement Workers of America (UAW), says: "My belief, based upon more than forty years as a worker, union member, and labor educator is that there is an increasing need for many and varied kinds of job skills to meet tomorrow's growing and challenging business and industry needs."

"The involvement by unions in training is both extensive and varied," adds Dorothy Shields, Director of the Department of Education of the AFL-CIO. "Programs which are national in scope reflect the commitment to help workers improve skills."

For further information on union apprenticeships and training, contact Department of Education, AFL-CIO, 101 Constitution Avenue, NW, Washington DC 20001.

DISTRIBUTIVE EDUCATION AND WORK-STUDY PROGRAMS

If you are still in high school, you may want to think of distributive education in which you attend school part time and spend the rest of your school day working for a business in your community.

Depending on what is available, you might work in such places as department stores; banks; pharmacies; travel agencies; municipal offices; credit companies; or air conditioning businesses, to mention a few possibilities. In one program, eight students were involved in fashion merchandising, and each afternoon they went to a major department store where they learned to run counters, create displays, prepare show windows, and design shopping bag logos. They were paid at least the minimum wage.

On the whole, distributive education programs get high marks from employers, and students often continue working after graduation. In fact, a national survey revealed that, when employers were asked to assess the importance of vocational education, more than half of the respondents said that their companies benefited from vocational education; 40 percent saw a benefit in lower training costs, while 60 percent reported that employees with a vocational education background require less training when they are hired. To find out more about distributive education, speak to your school advisor or write Distributive Education Clubs of America, 1908 Association Drive, Reston, VA 22091.

Community and two-year colleges offer work/study programs. Known as cooperative education, these programs give students a chance to dovetail their career and education as they work with participating employers. On many campuses cooperative education is available in accounting; automotive technology; commercial art; energy technology; hotel/restaurant management; laboratory technology; ornamental horticulture; communications; retail management; secretarial science; security and loss prevention; stage technology; computer science; banking; credit and finance; data processing; drafting and design; legal assistant training; and recreation. Usually students are paid for their work, but situations differ, so financial arrangements should be discussed.

Work/study programs are flourishing, and statistics show that nationally sixty percent of co-op students go to work permanently for their co-op employers after graduation. In Paramus, New Jersey, a graduate of Bergen Community College's Hotel and Restaurant Management Program made contact with the Marriott organization through cooperative education. At the end of the program, she was invited to stay on with the company and in less than a year she was promoted to Assistant Housekeeper at Marriott's hotel in Camelback, Arizona. In other cases, a media co-op student continued in a permanent production position at WNEW-TV in New York City, a student who worked with a drug chain was hired upon graduation to continue with the company full time. After setting up a store in a suburb he rose to become manager of the store and earn close to one million dollars in a year's business. Then, two years after his graduation, he became a manager in a branch that did a business of two million dollars per year.

For further information on cooperative education programs, contact the Cooperative Education Office of your area's community colleges.

INTERNSHIPS

"Intern programs are wonderful because if you want to learn to box the best way is to go into a ring and get your head beat in," believes Michael Levine, a young Hollywood publicist who has an intern program in his company. "An intern program takes away all sterile theories and shows what the actual work is about."

At one time internships were thought of as strictly for college students. But that has changed. In fact, Jane Kendell, executive director of the National Society of Internships and Experiential Education, stated in an article in *The New York Times:* "Internships are definitely growing in number and variety."

Some internships are paid, but more often they are not, as many people who enter the programs are willing to work for free to gain practical experience. For instance, as reported in *The New York Times* article, the Manhattan Theater Club in New York takes about thirty to forty interns every year. It accepts anyone who is interested in learning about theater and who is willing to make a full-time commitment, without any kind of payment. Sounds like a big contribution but, after three months, interns have gone on to become casting directors and business managers at other theaters.

For information on internships, write the National Society for Internships and Experiential Education, 124 St. Mary's Street., Raleigh, NC 27605. You can also consult *1985 INTERNSHIPS*, a helpful reference that contains over 16,000 opportunities for short-term, on-the-job positions in a wide variety of occupations. It is available at a nominal price from Writer's Digest Books, 9933 Alliance Road, Cincinnati, OH 45242.

ADULT SCHOOLS AND CONTINUING EDUCATION COURSES

Adult education classes in public schools and community colleges have a vast array of inexpensive courses that give you training for the marketplace. For instance, Michele Hogan Schmidt, the public relations director of the Sheraton New Orleans Hotel, took courses in journalism and media graphics while advancing her career. Charlene Margaritis, who also moved on the fast track in the public relations field, took short-term management courses. "It's what you get out of courses that counts and not how long they last," she asserted.

In addition to practical business skills, adult schools and continuing education programs offer courses in crafts and once you become proficient you can practice the craft. Sometimes, instead of learning a craft in a class situation, you can train by working alongside an established craftsperson. Take the case of Matthew Buechner, a studio glassblower with his own business who got his initial training by working without pay for a glassblower. The work interested him enough to take an independent college study course that included glass blowing. But he felt he was not learning much, so he dropped out of college.

"Instead I went to West Germany and worked as a helper in a glass shop making wine goblets," he reported in an interview in *Occupational Outlook Quarterly*. "In Germany, however, it takes 5 years of apprenticeship before you become a blower and 15 years of experience before you can become a master. This was longer than I wanted to wait."

With this decision behind him, Buechner returned to the United States and he and his brother opened a studio in Corning, New York. Later Buechner moved on to start a studio in Newport, Rhode Island.

HOME STUDY SCHOOLS

More than three million Americans are enrolled in home-study (or correspondence) courses, and admissions are increasing by approximately twenty-five percent every year. In a correspondence course, you study with an institution that provides you with lesson materials prepared in a sequential order. You mail assigned work back to the school for correction, grading, and guidance. Corrected assignments are returned to you.

Courses vary greatly. Some have few lessons and require only weeks to complete, while others have a hundred or more assignments requiring three or four years of study. For some home study courses the two-year associate's degree is awarded. The typical correspondence course can cost anywhere from $400 to $700, with some of the longer courses running considerably higher. As previously mentioned the National Home Study Council (NHSC) is the standard-setting agency for home study schools, so if you are interested in home study select a school with NHSC accreditation.

Home study students come from all walks of life. One famous example is Charles Schultz, the "Peanuts" cartoonist, who took a course, and later taught, at the Art Instructions School of Minneapolis, Minnesota. Another example is Nikolette Fadeff-Wood who enrolled in a course offered by the Gemological Institute of America. In twenty months, she earned the Graduate Gemologist Diploma (a course that normally requires at least three years) and, after receiving her diploma, began working as a sales clerk for a jeweler. In four months she was promoted to store manager. Later, in addition to doing the store's appraisal work and some jewelry designs, she began training some of the store's personnel and lecturing on gems.

Ernest "Buddy" Hardigree always dreamed of being a disc jockey. To get started, he enrolled in Columbia School of Broadcasting. He subsequently obtained a job as program director for WIMO radio station in Georgia. As program director he launched "Emergency Medical Service Week" to help inform the public of the emergency medical services available to them. For that program his station received the "Mass Media Award" for radio stations in Georgia.

If home study is the alternative for you, follow the procedures suggested for choosing a proprietary school. If you have specific questions about home study education or if you would like a copy of the NHSC Directory of Accredited Home Study Schools, write National Home Study Council, 1601 18th Street, NW, Washington, DC 20009.

THE VITAL QUESTION OF FINANCIAL AID

Depending on the type of training program you choose, there are opportunities for financial assistance available from a variety of sources. They include grants, loans, scholarships, and tuition payment plans offered by such sources as the Federal and state governments, foundations, corporations, and educational institutions.

Many people mistakenly think financial aid is only available for students attending four-year colleges and universities. But this is not the case as students enrolled in programs at two-year colleges and schools are also eligible for Federal student financial assistance. In fact, it has been estimated that about a third of the students in proprietary schools are in some loan program. Every school has a financial aid officer, so when you have two or three schools in mind, contact the financial aid office to determine what is available. A good first step in determining how much financial aid you will need is finding out how much your training will cost you.

The National Center for Education Statistics has prepared a booklet "Basic Student Charges, 2-Year Institutions" that provides a summary of student charges for more than 1300 public and private two-year colleges. Business and technical institutes are also included. It is available for $2.50 from the Superintendent of Documents, United States Government Printing Office, Washington, DC 20402.

Basically, there are three types of financial aid programs; grants, loans, and work study. The difference between grants and loans is that grants are outright awards to needy students enrolled in an accredited postsecondary school and do not have to be paid back. Loans, however, must be repaid within a specific period of time after schooling terminates. Despite suggested cuts and the ongoing controversy over how much — and to whom — aid should be given, the National Direct Student Loan Program and the Guaranteed Student Loan Program are the two major programs offered.

The Guaranteed Student Loan Program enables you to borrow from banks and other eligible lenders at a low interest rate to meet educational expenses, if you are attending a participating postsecondary school at least half time. Lenders may choose to whom they will lend, within GSL eligibility guidelines. In most states, loans are guaranteed by state or private nonprofit agencies. In states without these agencies, loans are insured by the Federal Government. Repayments for loans normally begin between nine and twelve months after you leave school, and you are generally allowed from five to ten years to repay the loan.

A third financial assistance program is work-study, which was discussed earlier in this chapter. Here the Federal government allots funds to help needy students earn part of their education expenses. Jobs are found for these students by the school. The employer pays a percentage of the hourly wage and the Federal Government pays the remainder.

Additional information on financial assistance programs can be obtained directly from schools, from the Bureau of Student Financial Assistance, P. O. Box 84, Washington, DC 20044, and from your state's department of education. You can also write to the Consumer Information Center, Department 518L, Pueblo, CO 81009 and ask for a copy of "Student Guide."

Still another helpful publication is "Need a Lift?" It is currently available for $1.00 prepaid — check or money order — from The American Legion, Emblem Sales, P.O. Box, 1050, Indianapolis, IN 46206.

If you are unable to obtain sufficient aid through the foregoing sources, the United States Aid Funds, Inc., a private, not-for-profit guarantee agency approved under the regulations of the United States Department of Education, offers a Vocational Loan Program. For further information, write to United Student Aid Funds, Inc., Program Development and Services, 8085 Knue Road, Indianapolis, IN 46250.

EMPLOYEE TRAINING PROGRAMS

If you pick the right employer, you may be able to get training after you get a job. Granted, some companies limit training to people with four-year degrees. But there is a readiness among other employers to provide job training and education to people who work at various levels. Lawrence A. Cremin, a retired president of Teachers College of Columbia University observed: "What they are saying to schools more and more is: 'Give us students who will come into the work force literate, and we'll teach them what they need to know throughout their careers.'"

A Bureau of Labor Statistics study underlined this fact when a survey of training in industry, based on a mailed questionnaire sent to 4,776 establishments in selected metal work industries, showed that employers provided training primarily because they felt job skills could best be taught in their own training programs.

In another survey on corporate education and training programs done by Seymour Lusterman for The Conference Board, Inc., a questionnaire sent to a sample of 2,798 companies, selected as representative of all United States firms having at least five hundred employees, showed that seventy-five percent of all companies provided some in-house courses for their employees. Eighty-nine percent had tuition-aid or refund programs, and seventy-four percent authorized some of their employees to take outside courses during work hours. Eleven percent of all employees took part in in-house courses, provided by their companies during working hours, and two percent were enrolled in company courses given during nonworking hours.

David Mier, now chairman of a thirty million dollar public relations company, found his natural talent for marketing and management when he got into the management training program of a company that sold farm equipment and accessories. "I muddled around and was in and out of college courses for a while after high school," he said. "But I never got my degree."

As an alternative, Mier entered the farm company's training program and worked for the firm for two or three years. Later the training he received allowed him to take advantage of other management opportunities and as he worked at these management jobs he found that not having a college degree was not that much of a drawback. "But I didn't particularly care for working for other people," he admitted, "so I always knew that someday I'd be an entrepreneur."

Mier's first entrepreneurship—and his move into marketing—was a Christmas-Gift-O-Rama. It was a fiasco, to say the least, and it left Mier and his partner $18,000 in debt. To get out of debt Mier took a trucking industry job at the management level. A few years later, his interest in auto racing prompted him, along with a friend, to form Racing Tours, Inc. to provide charter bus service from major cities to the races at Watkins Glen, New York.

"The 1972 oil embargo was on," he explained, "so we decided that if there was rationing our charter service would provide a way for spectators to get to the races."

This venture, like the Christmas-Gift-O-Rama, met with small success, because the embargo ended. But the project got Mier into other racing activities, and to complement his talent for management and marketing, in this new work he showed a flair for promotion. Consequently, after refining his skills on various promotional activities, he opened his own consulting firm. Later, he joined an advertising company where he started a public relations agency as one arm of the advertising firm. Within five years, while still in his thirties, he progressed to his present status. It all began with getting his start in a company training program.

LEARNING ON THE JOB WITHOUT EMPLOYEE TRAINING PROGRAMS

Many people who make it to the top begin with entry jobs and build their careers through learning on the job rather than through formalized training. Gerald Kern, for instance, never had the time or chance to learn through college courses or structured employee programs. But he *still* became president and chief executive officer of three burgeoning public companies.

Because his mother, who was on welfare, died two months before Kern finished high school, he had no financial resources for a college education. Instead, he enlisted in the Navy. Then, when he left the service, he went to work as a service station attendant for his older brother.

"Later we pooled a few thousand dollars and took a lease on a second service station," he declared. "But after working six and seven days a week sixteen and seventeen hours a day, I decided to look for something better."

The immediate "something better" was a job as a sales representative for the PET company and in the 6 years Kern worked in sales, he was so productive that the International Playtex Corporation recruited him to join the company as a management candidate at $12,000 per year. When Kern left the company—13 promotions later—he was president-general manager of a $35 million division and was making over $100,000 a year. After that meteoric success, he was lured to the cosmetics industry as a personal assistant to the chief executive officer of Max Factor. When he left that firm, he was vice-president of the United States division. He subsequently moved to the pharmaceutical industry to launch Meditech Pharmaceuticals, Inc. From that base, he established and financed a variety of other business ventures.

"The key to reaching job objectives is seeking recognition through accomplishment and making yourself very visible by putting in extra effort," he advised. "From the time I started working I proceeded to put in the full days, weeks, and months it takes to compete against individuals with better backgrounds, better educational experiences, and more job related experience than I had—and it paid off.

"You need to take advantage of every opportunity to learn what your job is and who the people who are most important to your career development are. If you ask yourself, 'What am I good at?' and 'Who do I know who can be influential in helping me accomplish my objective?' you have valuable answers to marketing your talents and skills."

SELF-EDUCATION

Finally, there is still another way to get at least part of the education that leads to a satisfying job and gives you what you want from life. It is called self-education!

"It strikes me there is a difference between education and learning," says environmentalist-journalist Michael Frome. "The former tends to be academic, theoretical, and hypothetical. Learning, on the other hand, is a self-assigned responsibility in which absolutely everything in life is factored into growth. Learning is sheer discovery, or the adventure of discovery.

"John Bartram, pioneer botanist of colonial times, began as a farmer, observing life-forms as he turned the soil. Though he had no one to teach him, he became botanist to the King and his house on the Schuylkill River was frequented by Benjamin Franklin, Thomas Jefferson, and other leaders of their time. Roger Tory Peterson has not been through college either, but he has 11 honorary degrees and the Presidential Medal of Freedom. He built his fame as an illustrator and self-taught naturalist around a simple but inspired system by which people could identify birds alive in the wild instead of dead on a specimen tray.

"On a visit to Dinosaur National Monument, outside Vernal, Utah, I met Tobe Wilkins," Frome added. "He has been working for twenty-five or thirty years as a preparator, using fine tools to outline the fossilized bones of ancient creatures embedded in rock. His work requires patience and knowledge. Yet he's a high school graduate who has taught himself paleontology and anatomy and who feels fullfilled in his career."

Another self-educated person is Louis L'Amour, the best-selling novelist of adventure stories covering Western frontier life. L'Amour left school at age fifteen and spent the next two decades traveling the world and taking whatever jobs he could find. During those years, he compensated for the formal education he lacked by reading in libraries all over the world and always carrying books with him.

As a result of his self-education he has become not only the author of more than 90 books, but also a geologist, ecologist, genealogist, cartographer, and historian. In 1983 in recognition of his work he became the first novelist in America to receive a special Congressional Gold Medal.

Often, when you choose an alternative to college, your specialized education eliminates liberal arts—those studies in colleges or universities intended to provide general knowledge, develop intellectual capacities, enrich your entire background, and keep you from being too narrow. However, with your public library as the university of the world, you do not have to go to college to educate yourself in liberal arts.

Instead read timely and timeless books, and learn about many subjects. Learn from people and from daily life experiences. Above all, make your learning an ongoing and lifelong project that will help you be all that you want to be for all the days of you life.

chapter eight

Marketing Strategies for Finding A Job

Twenty years ago Janice LaRouche was a thirty-seven-year-old divorcee with no job, no college education, and a five-year-old son to support. Today she is one of the most successful career counselors in America.

"It was out of my own story that I learned to counsel," she says. "When I had to go to work to support my child and myself I couldn't afford the time or money to go to school. I had to look for work with a future."

While Janice was looking for possibilities she stumbled across the title "Hospital Director of Volunteer Services." Because it was a helping profession that did not have rigid degree requirements, she thought it might be a potential for the future. She knew, however, that she could not begin with a job as a director, so she brushed up on her office skills and looked for a job with someone who had that title.

While she worked as a secretary, she considered herself a management trainee. For example, she taught herself how to write good letters and memos; gained experience in public speaking by participating in orientation seminars for new volunteers; and developed a managerial style by observing how her boss ran the hospital volunteer department.

"I looked for opportunities to do some of my boss's work," she wrote in her book *Strategies for Women at Work*. "The best way to do that, I found, was to see that she benefited from my taking over some of her activities."

In four years Janet negotiated three new job titles for herself—assistant to the director, assistant director, and associate director. This enabled her to join the Association of Hospital Volunteer Directors, which gave her enough visibility to be approached for jobs by several hospital administrators. She used this encouragement to apply for a job at an agency where she really wanted to work and, eventually, she reached the top of the director of volunteer services field.

Simultaneously, she became an activist in the National Organization for Women (NOW), and the career workshops she now runs professionally were originally a

NOW volunteer activity. When *The New York Times* wrote a story on her unique workshops, she received hundreds of calls and soon after that she struck out on her own and founded her New York-based Workshops For Women.

"It's your strengths that people want to buy," she declares. "The key thing is to be thoroughly convinced that you have a lot to offer. Often college is quite irrelevent. Your persuasion lies in showing how you can do the job."

By every standard, it is essential to convince employers you are the best possible person for a job—even without a four-year degree or some of the qualifications they say that they are seeking. Generally the tools and techniques you use will depend on the kind of job you want. Some will work for entry level or trainee jobs, while others will be needed for other types. Sometimes, without the four-year degree, you may have to use a back-door approach and prove yourself after you get inside.

According to a study by the Department of Labor, about fifteen percent of all job hunters find their jobs through a formal job-publicizing system—Help-Wanted ads, resumes, employment agencies, executive recruiters, and job banks. The rest find spots through other means, and some counselors who advise other means suggest job seekers circumvent employment agencies, personnel offices, and résumés. Career counselor John C. Crystal teaches people to avoid official job-publicizing channels and, instead, make contacts that get beyond personnel departments where, Crystal says, lack of appropriate background often means rejection.

"I'm not in the traditional mold," states Crystal, "and when people are told to depend upon the system I say 'Forget the system.' Almost to a person, people who don't have a college degree will feel 'I don't have a college degree and I don't have all the requisites.' But that is simply not true, though I believe anyone without a degree who is naive enough to put himself into the system is just cutting his own throat.

"The alternative is to discover what the reality is—and the reality is that personnel departments were invented to screen job seekers and keep them off the line manager's or supervisor's back. But the line manager or supervisor does the actual hiring, so my advice has always been to approach the one man or woman who has the most knowledge of the job you truly want and enough seniority to hire someone for it. Résumés are supposedly predictive tools, but when you add your résumé to the avalanche of others there's no guarantee that the offers you get will be for the job you want. When it comes to employment agencies they generally deal only with those people so easily packaged they fit a standard common denominator."

Crystal did not fit a common denominator when he began a job hunt after a World War II tour, where he served as a United States spy in Europe and North Africa. To begin with, he told the truth on his résumé: "1942–1946. U.S. Army, spy." Personnel directors laughed at him and someone advised him that he would be lucky to find any job at all. That did it, as far as Crystal was concerned. He took a look at the system and declared something was wrong with it.

With that decision behind him, he stopped haunting employment offices and figured out what he really wanted to do. The answer was to travel in Europe, as a civilian.

Because Crystal could speak seven languages, he began to think about what postwar Europe needed—and narrowed it down to items like shoes and stoves. Next, he needed a source of supply for the goods, so Crystal, age twenty-six at the time, decided to apply his spy techniques to find not only a firm he wanted to work with but also a person who would have the authority to judge his idea and hire him for the job. His choice was Sears Roebuck, and his target person was its chairman.

Before he made his pitch, he researched all facts of his idea and developed a plan and proposal that would show *specifically* how hiring him could benefit Sears Roebuck. It took eight days to get an appointment. But his efforts paid off when the chairman asked "How would you like to handle our European operations?"

Not everyone speaks seven languages and has comparable skills to Crystal. However, from his work in teaching and counseling, he is convinced people can bypass the system by being extremely specific about what they want to do and where they want to do it; working up a proposal identifying a need in a particular area and outlining how they think it can be met; going to the person who has the power to accept or reject the proposal; and getting to that person by making the right contacts.

To prove his point, Crystal cites the example of a high school graduate whose post-high school years were spent in jail rather than college. While in jail, the young man studied photography and became fascinated by photographic and printing equipment. His goal was to work in a print shop.

After his release from jail, he picked a town where he wanted to live and where he could ride to work on a bike. Next he read every library book he could find on the photographic equipment that interested him. After that, he investigated print shops and talked informally to people who worked in them. In his talks he was looking for a shop that had a good reputation and growth possibilities and used the photographic equipment that fascinated him. When he narrowed down the print shops to the one he really wanted to work for, he learned the name of the owner and found out the time of day the owner was relatively free.

When he went to the owner with his proposal, he presented himself as someone who had been trained on the kind of photographic and printing equipment the owner used in his shop. (Obviously, he did not say that he had been trained in jail.) Next, he built up more points when he spoke about riding his bike to work and getting in early in the morning and not rushing off at night. Then he finished by saying "I know quite a few people who run their own small business, and they all need printing from time to time. On my day off I'll visit my friends and drum up extra business."

"Needless to say he got the job," Crystal pointed out.

Job specialists and counselors seldom agree on marketing tools and techniques. Whether you choose a traditional or untraditional approach, the successful marketing of *you* calls for thoroughness and attention to detail, and many specialists still suggest you expose yourself to *all* of the tools. Those traditional and non-traditional tools follow in abbreviated form. For complete details, go to your library and read job-hunting books.

1. Establish your long-range objectives and decide where your opportunities will be.
2. Consult a career counseling service.
3. Line up potential employers.
4. Write letters to explore possibilities.
5. Talk to people and make many contacts.
6. Conduct "information interviews."
7. Go to personnel offices—if the job demands it.
8. Answer "Help Wanted" advertisements.
9. Register at employment agencies and placement offices.
10. Consider working for a temporary service.

ESTABLISH YOUR LONG-RANGE OBJECTIVES AND DECIDE WHERE YOUR BEST OPPORTUNITIES WILL BE

From some of your earlier evaluations, you have at least a general idea of your long-range objectives and what you have done and can do. Now is the time to review this again.

"Before I went into color analysis I asked myself 'What is the one thing I know a little bit about that I won't have to go to school for?'" Sherri Austin reported. "When I looked at the various things I'd done, I decided the cosmetics field would be the right objective."

"My first step was going to an employment agency," she revealed. "The agency could do nothing for me, but the interviewer knew a person he thought might help me and introduced us over the phone. That person had connections with the Max Factor Company, and when I was interviewed I was hired."

Sherri, by chance, landed a job in a large company. However, as previously noted, some of the best opportunities exist in smaller firms. "Often firms employing twenty or less people are run by entrepreneurs who couldn't care less about a piece of paper," Crystal stressed. "As opposed to walking in and saying 'I have a Harvard M.B.A.' you can walk in and show them what you can do."

CONSULT A CAREER-COUNSELING SERVICE IF YOU NEED IT

If you need help in marketing yourself, you may want to consult a reputable job-and-career counseling service. Unlike employment agencies and search firms, these services do not find jobs. Many of the highly competent ones offer solid advice and guidance, as well as programs that produce results.

As mentioned earlier, State Employment Agencies, service organizations (such as Ys), community colleges, career counseling organizations, and private counselors all provide evaluations. In some cases counseling is free; the majority charge a fee. Research services thoroughly and try to determine how much help the service has given to a substantial number of clients before signing up for counseling.

LINE UP POTENTIAL EMPLOYERS

As a starter, your local Chamber of Commerce can give you names and addresses of firms in your area. The Yellow Pages provide another source for lining up businesses; trade and professional organizations; nonprofit institutions; or government agencies. On library reference shelves you will find directories, such as Poor's Register of Corporations, that list firms in specific industries. Your daily newspaper will also give you clues to possible openings.

To find hidden job possibilities, read between the lines of news and business articles. Openings can result when new companies come to your area; branch offices are opened; mergers are reported; personnel is transferred; new buildings are planned; and contracts are awarded. The same thing is true when laws are passed; legislators are elected; and government changes from one party to another. Along with newspapers, trade publications publish reports of change in various fields.

List the firms and companies that interest you and note the name and title of the appropriate person to contact. This will get you started on a mailing list for a direct mail campaign. Learn all you can about a business's age, services, products, competitors, growth patterns, and reputation. Try to talk to employees to find out what they think of the business, what working there is like, and what their jobs entail.

WRITE LETTERS TO EXPLORE EMPLOYMENT POSSIBILITIES

As you compile a mailing list, send individual letters to the places on your list and direct each one to the specific person that you have noted. (Consult Chapter Nine for sample letters.) If you do not know the appropriate person, telephone the firm and ask the operator for the name of the person in charge of the work that interests you.

Because your letter is unsolicited, you have to convince someone that you can be an asset and are worth an interview. Do this by stating in a simple, direct way the kind of work you are interested in; credible reasons why you want to work for that business; and what you can do for it. Highlight your most outstanding credentials and qualifications, mention any training and experience that you have and request an interview on a specific or alternate date. State you will telephone at such-and-such a time for a date. There are many books in libraries that devote themselves exclusively to how-to-get-a-job letters. Study them carefully and use them as a guide.

Generally the percentage of returns in a direct mail campaign are small. Sometimes you get more response if, after waiting two weeks, you write a second letter (or make a telephone call). Say you are wondering if your letter was received, and whether you can set up an interview to learn about job opportunities, even if there are no openings at the time.

TALK TO PEOPLE AND MAKE MANY CONTACTS

Tell friends, relatives, community contacts and former employers that you are in the market for a job and ask for suggestions of possibilities. Reportedly, eighty percent of all jobs are filled through the grapevine.

"From the time I started working I made connections and did networking," explained Charlene Margaritis, while discussing her advertising and public relations career. "If I had an uncle who knew someone I called my uncle. If I had a friend who worked for somebody I called my friend."

"The more people you know, the more chances you have," added Barbara Brabec, the home business specialist. "I believe, like Max Gunther, author of *The Luck Factor*, that luck is something you catch by knowing a lot of people."

To get the most help from people, have questions prepared in advance. Ask such things as "How did you prepare yourself for your job?" "How do you like what you do?" and "What should I do to get into your field?" Ask for additional names of people to talk to, and when people help you write an immediate "Thank you."

CONDUCT INFORMATION INTERVIEWS AND FIND OUT WHO CAN HIRE YOU

John Crystal calls talking to people "information interviews" and, again, cites the story of the young man who investigated jobs in print shops. By talking informally to people who already worked in the shops, he was using "information interviews" to find out about the business; look for a need in his area of interest; and learn who to see who could hire him.

In another case, a graphic artist was interested in getting into the television field, but she had no college or TV experience. So what did she do? She talked with people involved in various aspects of television and discovered a need for artists to do on-screen computer graphics. Investigation indicated that a certain broadcasting company was hiring artists who had taken a particular manufacturer's three-day course. The graphic artist took the course and was immediately hired.

GO TO PERSONNEL OFFICES—
IF THE JOB DEMANDS IT

Although going directly to the person with the power to hire you is the ideal approach to a job, you are likely to face some situations where—speaking realistically—you have to go to a personnel office.

Before you start out, plan your answers to questions about your educational background and job experience. Be prepared to provide addresses and phone numbers of references and have a pen that is in good working order. If there is a question about salary on an application blank, write "Open" or "Negotiable." This can come up in the interview.

Résumés have become a controversial issue. If you plan to use one, carry a pocket stapler with you and staple your résumé to your application blank.

ANSWER "HELP WANTED" ADVERTISEMENTS

About eighty percent of job openings are never advertised, so how helpful ads turn out to be will depend, to a large extent, on the job you seek. Along with newspapers, trade publications and professional journals run job ads. Many will be in your local library. Most libraries also have the *Standard Rate and Data Directory of Business Magazines* and the index of this directory lists the names and addresses of publications. If publications are not in your library, you can send to the publishers for copies.

When answering "Help Wanted" ads seems right for you, answer by phone or letter. If asked to submit a letter and résumé use the example in Figure 8-1, written by a non-college graduate. All names, institutions, dates, and

FIGURE 8-1

November 1, 1984

Mr. John Jackson, Catering Director
ABRAMS & PARKER
211 Main Street
Cooperstown, N.Y. 13326

Dear Mr. Jackson:

Your advertisement for an experienced chef's assistant in The Town Crier on Wednesday, October 31, interests me a great deal since my background and working experience are very much in line with your needs. I have been involved in catering in every job I've held, and this is an aspect of the food service business I particularly like. I was especially commended for the high-pressured and successful catering I did when St. Joseph's food service staff catered the 12th Annual Tennis Tournament last summer.

As you will see by my attached resume I am currently employed by St. Joseph's Seminary as an assistant chef. After five years in this job I am looking for a new opportunity with growth potential since the enrollment at the Seminary is becoming smaller each fall. I can be available for employment as soon as I give the Seminary the standard two weeks' notice. As I'm a Cooperstown resident, I'm conveniently located to Abrams & Parker.

(continued)

FIGURE 8-1, continued

I have had courses in catering and food service at Atlantic Community College, plus ten years of solid experience in the field. Since Monday, November 5, is my day off from work I would like very much to have an appointment for an interview on that day if it fits your convenience. If this day is not convenient I can come in on Friday, the 9th at 9:00 or 9:15 A.M. since I am not due to work till 11:00 that day.

I will call you prior to November 5 to see if we can set up an interview. I can be reached at 920-7562, and messages will be taken for me if I am not there.

Thank you very much.

        Sincerely,

        Bruce Baylor

275 Second Avenue
Cooperstown, N.Y. 11326

places have been changed. Before the applicant wrote his letter, he checked out the advertiser and when he learned it was a catering firm he stressed his catering experience. (His résumé appears in Chapter Nine.) He also telephoned Abrams & Parker to ask for the name of the catering director. Here is the ad he answered.

> CHEF'S ASSISTANT—Experience required. Full-time position. Excel oppt. Reply with resume to ABRAMS & PARKER, Cooperstown, NY 13326.

REGISTER AT EMPLOYMENT AGENCIES AND PLACEMENT OFFICES

Junior and community colleges, as well as vocational, technical, and business schools, often have placement services, so, if you have attended one, take advantage of its help.

Usually private employment agencies are most helpful when you know precisely what you want and when an agency specializes in a particular field. Before registering with one, call employers in your job field and ask which agencies they use. You can also evaluate agencies by the ads they run. For instance, when an agency places an ad for the same job again and again, you can conclude the employer who placed the job order probably has a terrific turnover and would not be a good potential. An ad that promises too much and sounds too good is another negative, so ads like "Super boss seeks superior secretary for superlative office" should make you run in the other direction from the agencies that place those ads. Above all, when you register, read all the fine print about fees before you sign a contract.

Your state employment service is still another job-hunting potential, but, because the service is free, state offices are usually crowded and understaffed. Many of the openings are for lower-salary, entry jobs—although sometimes there are leads to technical and semiprofessional occupations. The state employment service, also called the Job Service, is under the direction of the Labor Department's United States Employment Service.

Many state employment services are now tied into a Job Bank program in which listings of openings from several states are fed into a computer and updated every day. To find your nearest state employment or Job Service office, look in the state government telephone listings under "Employment Services" or "Labor Department."

CONSIDER WORKING FOR A TEMPORARY EMPLOYMENT SERVICE WHILE LOOKING FOR WHAT YOU WANT

This is a good way to make contacts and earn money while marketing yourself because temporary work offers job opportunities in a variety of fields. For example, one of the largest services—The Olsten Corporation under its trade names Olsten Temporary Services and Olsten Health Care Services—has 280 offices throughout the United States and Canada. Its 9 classifications include: office services; health care services; office automation; accounting services; light industrial services; records management services; legal support services; marketing services; and SemiTech services.

While temporary employment provides you with experience and gives you an overview of work, it has the added benefit of letting you buy time while you continue to market yourself for the permanent employment that fits your interest. As job counselor Richard Irish put it when discussing temporary jobs, "Hanging in and looking for your job is a far better way to spend a year than punching a time clock in an organization you despise. If you don't believe *now* that you can find the job, you'll be postponing—perhaps forever—the possibility that a job can be anything more than a meal ticket."

_____chapter nine

Résumés, Letters, And Interviews

Some job specialists maintain that "résumés advertise you and your skills," while others reject the résumé in favor of other approaches. "Résumés don't open doors—people do," insists guru John Crystal, who favors "talking résumés" during the interview.

"I don't see the big problem about a résumé," counters counselor Janice LaRouche. "Why not have one if someone wants it? You have to have some summing-up to offer, whether it's a résumé, a wrap-up letter, or a statement of your background."

"I think the most important thing is to have a sequence of experience," concludes Ronald Pilenzo, president of the American Society for Personnel Administration. "But keep it brief, and write every single word with caution. I don't believe in mailing out 500 résumés. That will get you nowhere. What you have to do is pick out half a dozen places and send your résumé directed to the person who could help you in that firm. Then don't wait for someone to call you. That will seldom happen. Instead call up the company and say 'I mailed you a résumé two weeks ago. I'm going to be in your neighborhood, and I'd like to meet with someone to talk about my résumé.'"

However you feel about résumés—or whatever view you accept—there will definitely be occasions when you will be expected to provide one. How you put it together will depend on your background and experience and the type of job you are seeking. Your library will have some excellent books devoted to writing résumés.

PLANNING YOUR RESUME

To get started, return to earlier chapters and refresh yourself on your interests and background. Once again, write down every accomplishment in your life that made you feel effective. Try to spot patterns and identify marketable skills. As you reaffirm patterns, put the skills that fit each pattern into special headings—for example, leadership skills, budget management skills, organization skills, whatever. Then, after you have your lists of headings, start drafting your résumé.

WRITING YOUR RESUME

Any work experience (no matter how minimal) should be part of your résumé because the fact that you have worked shows you as a go-getter rather than a person who is dragging his or her feet.

"Put down anything you can think of that you did," advises Ronald Pilenzo. "If you were a sales clerk in a jeans store you might say *'Participated in inventories of the entire store every month; made recommendations on the product lines; organized the back room; helped close the books at the end of the month.'* This gives you an edge over someone who puts down 'I was a sales clerk for X company for 2 years.'

"The same thing is true of volunteer and community work," he went on. "When you have no degree you may want to put down a paragraph about this work as a way of showing you're a well-rounded person and have other relevant skills to transfer to a job."

If you have taken evening or continuing education college courses list the name of the college and specify "Intensive course in _____" or "Short-term course in _____." Similarly, if you attended college as an undergraduate and then decided to leave, indicate the college experience. Just do not imply that you graduated.

You can use the sample of a chronological résumé shown in Figure 9-1 as a guide. It was prepared by the non-college graduate developing a career in food service. As in the previous chapter, all names, institutions, dates, and places have been changed.

A functional résumé, as opposed to a chronological one, concentrates on what you have done and does not always pinpoint places and dates, so if you are short on job experience the functional résumé may be a good choice. Employers will respect accomplishment and skills

FIGURE 9-1

BRUCE BAYLOR

275 Second Ave.   607-920-7562   Cooperstown, N.Y. 13326

Objective: FOOD SERVICE - CHEF

WORK EXPERIENCE
<u>Assistant Chef</u>, St. Joseph's Seminary, Cooperstown, N.Y. 1980– Present

> Helped food service manager plan meals and participated in the preparation of meats, vegetables, sauces, and other foods; cooked lunch and dinner meals for students and faculty; introduced a variety of new homemade soups for lunch; selected new recipes and developed new items for dinner menu; prepared special meals for the many retreats and meetings held at the Seminary; catered faculty parties and other special events; saw that dishes were garnished and presented in a tasteful and attractive way; estimated food consumption and checked food for quality and quantity; helped requisition and purchase food in large quantities and assumed full responsibility for this when food service manager was away; cut, trimmed, and boned meats and poultry; handled the correct storage of new and leftover foods.

<u>Chef</u>, Davis & Davis Food Service, Edison College, Susquehanna, NY   1978–1980

> Prepared all soups and entrees for lunch. Also prepared food for catered affairs, buffets, and special events. Assisted in planning cycle menus; introduced new soups and entrees; ordered food.

<u>Assistant Chef</u>, Mount Saint Johns Villa, Syracuse, N.Y. 1976–1978

> Helped chef prepare dinners (noon). Full responsibility for preparing suppers. Assisted in planning meals. Responsible for preparing breakfast, dinner, and supper when chef was off. Had complete charge of all food service during long period while chef was ill

FIGURE 9-1, continued

<u>Assistant Chef</u>, Holland Haven, Geneva, N.Y.   1974–1976

During 1974–1975 had full charge of employee meals and breakfasts for guests. Helped chef prepare guests' dinners. In 1976 we were a resort and gourmet restaurant. I was in charge of special buffets and breakfasts and dinners for resort guests. Helped chef prepare gourmet restaurant meals. During my three years here I helped plan all menus for resort guests and was in charge of ordering foods.

<u>Cook</u>, Atlantic Country Day School, Atlantic City, N.J.   1970–1973

<u>SUMMER AND PART-TIME EMPLOYMENT</u>
<u>Cooking and Meal Preparation 1967–1970</u>

    High Mountain House, Lake Placid, N.Y.
    Steak Pub, Rumson, N.J.
    The Golden Eagle, Atlantic City, N.J.

<u>EDUCATION</u>
    Atlantic High School 1966–1970
    Atlantic Community College, Short-term evening food service courses 1972

<u>PERSONAL</u>
Born 1952. Excellent health. Single. Highly responsible—only 2 days' absenteeism in 5 years.

REFERENCES ON REQUEST

because they know these accomplishments are achieved by action, ingenuity, and energy. When you focus on volunteer work, describe it as you would describe a paid job. Here are some examples from functional résumés:

From a dental assistant and office manager who wanted to move to a higher-level office management job in the health field:

ORGANIZATIONAL SKILLS: As an office manager, I organized and supervised the daily

SAMPLE RÉSUMÉ

Mary Anne Smith
123 Elm Street
Newfield, Indiana 45678
Telephone: 123-4567

VOCATIONAL OBJECTIVES

Customer relations manager or administrative assistant. Qualified for a position that requires communication and management skills.

SUMMARY OF BACKGROUND

Attended Indiana University and studied business administration in night classes, specializing in business application of computer science. •

Worked for three years as secretary to manager of sales division, ABC Company. Was promoted to administrative assistant, and coordinated schedules and data flow for forty-five salespeople. Left to raise two children. During last ten years, coordinated annual United Fund drive in my neighborhood. •

MANAGEMENT SKILLS

Organized ninety volunteer fundraisers into statewide taskforce for United Fund's Golden Anniversary drive, which raised $375,000 and exceeded any previous year's contribution by 20 percent. As member of day-care-center board, helped revamp federal funding guidelines, increased community participation on board, and headed search committee that hired new director. Revamped salesman-husband's chaotic filing system so that part-time and tempo-

---

NOTES:

1. She went to college for only one semester, but who cares? If anybody does, they can check.

2. At forty-two, she's had only three years of salaried employment, but by focusing on her achievements in that job and in volunteer work, she presents herself as competent and productive—which she is!

4. Any initiative that leads to concrete results is of interest to smart employers. It doesn't have to involve millions of dollars.

5. Even the things you do for pleasure teach certain skills.

3. Though her interest in computers was largely motivated by a need to assist her husband in his business, she wisely recognizes that any skill she's picked up may be marketable.

rary employees could understand it, and oversaw installation of microcomputer in his office. •

MONEY MANAGEMENT SKILLS

Have consistently managed a tight family budget so that we annually save 10 percent of our income. When I received a small inheritance, I studied investing and invested it for a 20 percent annual return. To raise money for son's class trip, devised scheme whereby all class parents agreed to collect moneyback supermarket coupons; raised the necessary $500 in two months. •

COMPETITIVE AND TEAM SKILLS

An avid athletic participant, I've finished among first twenty women runners in local marathon for past five years. Organized a bridge club of players who love the game for its analytical qualities and am usually top scorer out of eight players. Sing in church choir for pleasure of the music and collaborative effort. •

PERSONAL DATA
Available: August 1
Birthdate: November 20, 1941 •
Family: married, mother of two sons in high school
Travel: willing to travel for short periods of time

REFERENCES
John Doe, state chairman, United Fund: 123-4567
Jane Williams, Ph.D., director Village Day Care Center: 765-4321

6. Unlike some, I advise giving your birthdate. Trying to conceal your age says more about you than stating the truth. But since age discrimination is real and rampant, you might bury this—and give just your birthdate. Some employers won't even bother to figure out how old you are today.

From "How to Write a Winning Resume" by Richard Irish, *Woman's Day*, May 17, 1983, Reprinted by permission.

functions of the office. I conducted consultations, interviewed new patients, and took charge of all the bookkeeping and accounts. This resulted in a more efficient use of time and secured the payment of outstanding debts.

From a waitress who wanted a job as an assistant banquet manager:

PERSUASIVE SKILLS: In the hospitality field I developed a steady clientele. Because of my services and recommendations to this executive-level clientele, the hotel has received many bookings for large corporate functions.

From a district sales supervisor applying for a spot as regional sales manager:

SUPERVISORY SKILLS: As a supervisor I assist in the interviewing and hiring of employees and help them organize their offices, territories, and time. My success is shown in the significant increases in the revenue they are providing for the company.

Figure 9-2 shows a functional resume suggested by Richard Irish, with his analysis of how a non-college graduate with limited working experience can present herself.

The care that goes into preparing your résumé shows your respect for yourself—and for your work—so see that it is error-free. This will be a plus in your favor as so many applicants are careless about details that matter. Says Gary A. Mainor, Director of Human Resources for the WCB Group: "I've looked at many college résumés that were a mess—misspelled words, incorrect grammar, et cetera. Some non-college graduates' résumés sold themselves better and got people to an interview that resulted in a job."

COUNTERACTING "YOU HAVE NO EXPERIENCE"

"This can be a Catch-22 situation," says Ronald Pilenzo, "so you have to be prepared to handle it. One way is to be so convincing a prospective employer can sense that if he will give you a chance you're literally willing to do anything to get the opportunity to prove yourself.

"In addition, try and make a correlation between the job for which you're applying and other experience you've had. Here's where the volunteer work comes in, since it can show organizing, fund-raising, and marketing ability, plus a whole range of other skills. Military experience is another thing that's valuable."

Gerald Kern, the executive from the pharmaceutical industry, found the way to get over the "no experience" hurdle when he was interviewed for a sales representative's job and then rejected for lack of experience.

"Instead of accepting that rejection I called the vice-president of sales and applied for the job again," stressed Kern. "I told him that if his company had the need for someone with basic intelligence who would be dedicated to getting the job done, I was their man."

Kern went on to tell the vice-president that it was true he had no experience. But if nobody gave him a job, he said, he would *never* have any experience. His reasoning and persistence got him the job that launched a dynamic career.

LETTERS

Many résumés are directed to a general audience. Consequently, you need an individualized cover letter written to a specific person for each résumé you send out. The purpose of the letter-plus-résumé is to get you an interview by drawing attention to accomplishments that relate to the immediate benefits you can contribute to a business. It is ideal to point out specific problems you can help an employer solve.

FIGURE 9-3

BRUCE BAYLOR
275 Second Ave.
Cooperstown, N.Y. 13326
607-920-7562

September 25, 1984

Mr. John Jacobs, Food Service Director
M. B. Montague Foods
272 Broadway
Brielle, N.J. 08730

Dear Mr. Jacobs:

For the past 10 years I have had solid experience in the food service business. For most of that time I have worked in institution feeding, and since my interest now lies in that area of the business I am anxious to stay in institutional work. My resume is attached.

Currently I am employed as assistant chef by St. Joseph's Seminary, but since the enrollment at the seminary is becoming smaller each fall, I am looking for a new opportunity. I have read that you are expanding and opening new cafeterias and executive dining rooms in New Jersey, so since I am anxious to work for a company where there is growth potential, I'd very much like to talk with you about employment possibilities. I am single and free to relocate.

In institutional feeding my work has included, among other things, helping plan and prepare meals; introducing new foods; catering special events; estimating food consumption; helping requisition and order foods and, in some cases, having full charge of ordering; checking foods for quality and quantity; and handling correct storage of foods.

I will be in your area on Tuesday, October 2, and Wednesday, October 3. Can we set a date for an interview at a time that's convenient with you on one of those days? I will phone you on Monday, October 1, to see what time is good for you. I look forward to talking with you.

Sincerely,
Bruce Baylor

FIGURE 9-4

Mary Anne Smith
123 Elm Street
Newfield, Indiana 45678
888-123-4567

September 25, 1984

Mr._____
Vice President, Customer Relations
_____
_____

Dear Mr._____:

Sylvia Reynolds has suggested that I contact you regarding a job as an administrative assistant or assistant manager in your customer relations department. I feel especially well-equipped to help expedite some of your workload because my administrative and management accomplishments have included the following:

- As administrative assistant to the manager of sales division for ABC company, I coordinated schedules and data flow for forty-five salespeople.

- As director of volunteers for United Fund's Golden Anniversary drive, I organized ninety volunteer fundraisers into a statewide taskforce that raised $375,000. This exceeded any previous year's contribution by 20 percent.

- As a member of a day-care-center board, I helped revamp federal funding guidelines, increased community participation on board, and headed a search committee that hired a new director.

- As an assistant to my salesman-husband, I organized his filing system so part-time and temporary employees can understand the system. I also oversaw the installation of a micro-computer in his office.

(continued)

FIGURE 9-4, continued

I attended Indiana University and studied business administration in night classes, specializing in business application of computer science. As a result I am anxious not only to work in this area but also to take ongoing courses that will help me assist in your computer-related activities.

I am confident I can make a worthwhile contribution to your customer relations department, so I would appreciate the opportunity to meet with you next week. I'll call your secretary to set up an appointment.

Sincerely,

Mary Ann Smith

The sample individualized letter in Figure 9-3 was attached to the résumé of the person seeking the food service job. Instead of answering a "Help Wanted" ad, he was sending his résumé to a company that was expanding.

Sometimes instead of a letter-plus-résumé, you may want to write a customized résumé-substitute letter. Says John Crystal: "I've seen too many people flip through a stack of résumés and then throw them out to believe in résumés as a practical tool, unless they're in the form of a personal letter."

Figure 9-4 shows a hypothetical letter that Mary Anne Smith—the nondegree woman who wrote the sample functional résumé—might have written as a résumé-substitute letter.

As you can see by these samples of résumés and letters, you never mention your salary history or your desired salary in résumés, cover letters, or résumé-substitute letters. It cannot be stressed enough that the time for a salary discussion is during an interview.

"You also avoid waving a flag like 'While I haven't been able to complete college...,'" warns Janice LaRouche. "That is one of the mistakes I see most often in cover letters. Rather than writing long sentences about what you don't have, you write what you do have. You say, 'I have this-and-that skill,' and you talk about relevant accomplishments."

Not every résumé and letter you send will result in interviews. But you should get some yeses, and when an appointment is set up you are on your way to the most critical moment in marketing yourself.

INTERVIEWS

"The things that count in interviews are (1) your ability to articulate what you want, (2) a good presentation of how you think you can do the job, and (3) your physical appearance," says Ronald Pilenzo.

"Too many people go into an interview, give the interviewer their application, and then just sit there and wait for the interviewer to ask a series of questions to which they answer 'Yes' or 'No,'" continued Pilenzo. "You can have a whole interview with half a dozen 'Yeses' and 'Nos' and it will be over before you figure out what is going on.

"Naturally you have to be sure interviewers get the answers to their questions," he went on. "But you should never leave until you've asked your questions, too. You create a favorable impression when you ask the right questions. These questions will show you do in-depth thinking, and as you get your answers you'll learn a great deal about a company and the way it sees its employees."

Before interviewers start their side of the questioning, try to find out what the most important responsibilities of the job are. "It's critical to learn as much about the job from the interviewer as you can," comments Pilenzo. "Then you can quickly make an analogy of the job requirements and how your experience relates to the job."

Throughout the interview, keep highlighting the abilities and skills that qualify you for the job. However, be sure you do not do so much talking the interviewer will feel you are interviewing him and taking over his role.

WHAT ABOUT SALARY?

Some career counselors believe in asking about salary, wages, and the total compensation package early in the interview. Others advise postponing this subject until later in the discussion. You will have to use your own judgment, but it is highly probable that interviewers will ask point blank, "What salary do you expect?" Counter with (1) "Naturally, I want to earn as much as I can, but rather than stating a specific figure, I'd prefer to rely on your sense of fairness," (2) "I'd like to leave the question of salary open until we've finished discussing every detail about the job," or (3) "What is the range for this job?"

This hedging should work. If you get into a bind and have to state a figure, quote a salary range. Sometimes an employer may insist on asking what your previous salary history was, and this can be hard to answer if in a former job or jobs you earned a substandard salary. Generally, the best response is "I took a low salary for the job because I liked the work and believed that I would have a good opportunity to learn and develop in the job. But as time went on, I realized that the chance wasn't there."

"BUT YOU DON'T HAVE A COLLEGE DEGREE"

There is no doubt that you will hear this statement along your job-hunting route, so whenever a question about college comes up, it is vital to emphasize experience over education. Says Gary Mainor, the previously quoted Director of Human Resources, "If people are competing with college graduates for a job that requires a degree, applicable experience would be a must."

John Crystal points out that if an employer has stipulated credentials or degrees it is often because these stipulations are his only way of conveying leadership qualities. "But he's not interested in degrees themselves so much as in the person he feels is likely to have them," contends Crystal. In his book *28 Days To A Better Job*, employment specialist Tom Jackson suggests that if an employer says that you do not have the education for the job you should counter with, "I know it looks that way on the surface. Actually if we were to work together you would see how my direct experience has more than compensated for this."

If you attended college and left, many interviewers will be sure to ask, "Why didn't you finish college?" You will sound both credible and honest if you say "Economic necessity," or "Needed at home for a family crisis." It is wise to add that you would like to take courses that will help you with your job.

"I believe very strongly that it's good to have 'Some college' on your résumé," re-emphasized Joseph Nicolato, the senior vice president at Volvo. "When I see 'Some college' that tells me that applicant has demonstrated enough self-discipline to handle homework assignments and study for tests and that's important to me in business. That's all college means to me, and that's the end of it. In the absence of 'Some college' you can tell me what your accomplishments have been.

"But more than anything else I want to see desire and enthusiasm. Formal education is an acquired skill. But you can't acquire enthusiasm and desire. You're born with those ingredients. I can give you the other skills."

Charlene Margaritis, who has interviewed and hired people in her advertising and public relations career, also feels enthusiasm must come across in an interview. "As far as the degree goes, I'd say never bring it up yourself," she said, "because you never know what your interviewer's feelings about college may be.

"However, if lack of college does come up as a perceived shortcoming, turn it into a positive by saying 'Because I entered the business world at a younger age, I have four more years of working experience. I'm bringing experience I don't think any college can give—or certainly didn't give at the time I could have applied.' You can also say you were hungry to start working and learn by doing. And sometimes you can reason with, 'Look at this list of credentials that I was able to accumulate in the four years college would have taken.'

"In one interview where I said I had attended college, I was pressed to say for how long," she acknowledged, "and when I answered apologetically the interviewer reacted by saying, 'You never have to be ashamed that you didn't finish. It's a credit to you that you've come this far.' That really changed my attitude about not having a degree and, instead of being ashamed that I didn't have it, I became proud of what I had done without it. Later, when people came to me for interviews for jobs in departments I headed, I always judged them more on experience than on the school they attended."

"I think people get overly concerned with the interviewer's questions about college," adds Janice LaRouche. "Instead of thinking independently about what the work really consists of and then selling their abilities and qualifications, they get intimidated by not being what the other person wants them to be.

"The big secret is to be non-defensive—and if you've done your homework and figured out whether you can do the job, you *will* be non-defensive and convinced you have a lot to offer. You have to have a belief in yourself and in what you have to sell."

IV

HOW TO MOVE UP ONCE YOU'VE MOVED IN

chapter ten

Moving Up and On

"My decision not to go to college was placed upon me by my family," said publicist Diane Hannan. "After high school, I did not have enough drive to finance my own way through or even realize that could be accomplished. What I did have were basic skills, and the attitude that I would always do more than what was expected of me. Because of this attitude, I had a chance to work at many jobs and learn a variety of skills."

The drive that was lacking after high school developed as Diane taught herself by reading extensively.

"I also attended seminars," she recalled, "and I especially remember taking a Dale Carnegie seminar which my employer paid for and, then, obtaining so much confidence through that seminar that I requested a raise. When the raise was denied I quit my job, knowing I could always move on to a better job."

Building credentials for moving on is what first jobs are for, so, as you set long-range life goals, explore ways to implement them. "Create a broad timetable for reaching them, but at the same time set some immediate objectives as part of your long-range goals," advises John Crystal.

"Just because you don't have a college degree doesn't mean you shouldn't have a personal game plan," declares Joseph Nicolato. "You need to develop a five-year plan within your present organization or, if you can't go further without a college degree, through a move to another place."

Because early jobs are not your limit, here are things to keep in mind for developing your personal game plan.

MAINTAIN A GOOD ATTITUDE

Dr. William E. Lacey, an associate professor in the United States International University School of Business and Management (and a person who has worked in management in his own construction business and as sales manager for a major corporation), believes attitude, rather than a person's innate talent, is the most important part of being a good employee.

"People can be taught if they have the right attitude toward accepting teaching and learning," he reasons. "But employees who say to themselves, 'Hey, they're going to teach me to do something new' are never going to be valued workers."

As part of the right attitude, offer positive suggestions rather than criticism of company policies and find out exactly what the company expects as an output from your job. A good way to know for sure is to ask your supervisor. "That indicates a real interest in the job if you try to match the company's expectations," says Lacey.

REACH OUT TO NEW LEARNING OPPORTUNITIES

The need to continuously improve yourself cannot be highlighted enough, so look at the constant pursuit of learning as a life-long triangular structure with job-skill training on one point, and personal development and social skills at the other two points.

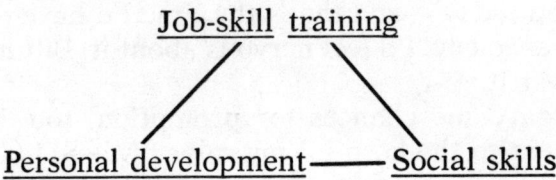

If, for one reason or another, you feel shortchanged in social skills and wish you had more finesse, polish the rough edges through a self-study course on manners, speech, amenities, and decorum. Good etiquette and polished speech count *for* you in moving ahead, while careless English and lack of good manners put you way behind. In one case, a man who did not recognize his shortcomings in language and speech was passed over for a promotion because his boss could not tolerate his "me and you" and his "comin' " and "goin'."

In another situation, a woman who was getting nowhere in her current job answered an ad for a sales representative and, as part of the job interview, was taken out for lunch. She constantly talked with food in her mouth and picked up a whole slice of bread and literally smeared it with butter. The person doing the interview crossed the woman off the list because of her poor manners and lack of social amenities.

GET A MENTOR

A mentor can make a big difference, so if someone shows an interest in teaching and guiding you, take advantage of the guidance. Often the best person is a boss who sees your potential.

"My mentor was the person I worked for in my first job at a hospital," commented Sharon Morgan, the vice president of an advertising firm. "He'd always explain everything that was happening, and he'd make me do things so I'd learn."

"Sometimes we'd go to meetings and he'd say 'I'll be calling on you, so I want you to be prepared.' Then he wouldn't call on me. Other times he'd announce 'I won't call on you today'—and that's the time I'd have to speak extemporaneously. I'd feel nervous about it. But he made me get over it.

"He gave me chances for promotion, too, because when I went to the hospital my salary was $11,000. Five years later it was $30,000."

CONTINUE SEEKING HELP FROM OTHER PEOPLE

We have already stressed the value of networks and establishing contacts with people. Neither can be emphasized enough because of the sizeable role they play in moving up and on. A good network will bring you in contact with people who share your situation and problems, and in return for the help you get you will contribute your knowledge, also. Joining or establishing a network often takes some time, but when you join organizations and attend conferences, meetings, and seminars, you will develop and improve contacts.

Even when you are not in a network, you can create your own way to build contacts. In "The Art of Getting Hired" in *18 Almanac*, a 13-30 Corporation publication, Harry Slonaker relates the story of a 26-year-old man who never went to college but who worked up to making $30,000 per year as an engineer for one of the biggest railroads in the country. When the young man tried to enter a craft after high school, he could not break into the ranks of any union. Because he was unable to do this, he joined the railroad as a laborer, only to find that time after time he was passed over for promotions in deference to workers with older relatives in the company. At that point he went to a district manager and told him that even though he was doing a good job, he felt he was getting cheated because he had no relatives who were working for the railroad. Soon after he established his contact, he was made a brakeman. Later, the railroad sent him to engineering school. "If you don't already know anyone who is going to help you," he advised, "you'd better find someone. If you muster a little courage, you can do just that."

DEVELOP GOOD "PEOPLE SKILLS"

Your ability to get along with people will be another determining factor in how you move up in your work. Except for extreme situations when the "difficult person" problem is so unfair and intolerable the only solution is to move, work smoothly with people of all ages and levels, regardless of how you feel toward them. You will encounter some impossible situations, of course. If you can rise above personality conflicts and keep away from hassles, someone who can help you progress is bound to notice your "People Skills."

One of the most valuable "People Skills" is listening and making people feel important. Many people make the mistake of blocking people out, and when others cannot get through to you it follows that it is hard to get through to them.

Dr. Lyman K. Steil, a listening expert who has aided

in the listening development of thousands of individuals throughout the United States, Canada, and Europe, says: "Eight major studies conducted over a period of fifty years with a diverse subject population have resulted in the unchallenged conclusion that listening is the primary communication activity utilized daily by the average individual. Without question, listening has been found to be central to the personal, social, educational, and professional success of every individual."

ASK FOR RESPONSIBILITY

Constantly show your employer that you have what it takes to do the task normally assigned to people with a four-year degree. For example, if a job comes up, go after it without waiting to be asked if you want it. Or, if openings do not occur, present a proposal to your employer that defines a new and more challenging job that you could handle for him.

"In all of my jobs I asked for more responsibility," explained Barbara Brabec, the home business specialist. "I'd say 'I've come to this place to work, so give me as much as possible because I want to learn. Every time I'd accomplish something I'd say 'Okay, that was easy. Now give me something more difficult.' In your career development you have to voice what you can do."

If you hope that added responsibility will get you into management, you will need to develop leadership qualities and supervisory skills. This will involve, among other things, showing expertise in planning and delegating work; dealing with pressure and conflict; making tough and fast decisions; managing people; rejecting poor work; and taking necessary risks.

You will also have to be a problem solver and find solutions yourself instead of looking for someone above you to solve the problems that come up each day. Courses and seminars with titles such as "Fundamentals of Management and Supervision," "A Manager's Guide to Human

Behavior," and "Planning and Control for Managers" are frequently given at community colleges.

MANAGE YOUR TIME AND YOURSELF

Getting yourself and your time organized are two other factors that make you productive and determine the quality of your life.

"Good organization is a set of methods that maintain control," asserts Stephanie Winston, founder and director of The Organizing Principle and author of *Getting Organized*. "You find what you want. You get done what you want to get done when you want to get it done. And in a day-to-day sense you live the life that gets you where you want to go."

"For the sake of being productive and making the most of your life, ask yourself constantly, 'How perfectly does this have to be done?'" adds Sunny Schlenger, director of Schlenger Organizational Systems. "Many tasks must be 'A' jobs. But we get hung up on other things that needn't be absolutely perfect and that prevents us from moving on to jobs that are better payoffs. In school we were used to aiming for 'A's in everything we did. But in the work world it's different. All the tasks have to be balanced, one against the other."

Above all, finish what you start instead of leaving loose ends. Edwin Bliss, author of *Getting Things Done* and head of his own management consulting business, underscores the need to force yourself to complete a job rather than getting it ninety-five percent finished. "Somebody compared this to baseball and said you don't get any credit for getting a guy to third base," he declared. "You have to go to home plate to score."

COME UP WITH INNOVATIVE IDEAS

You will get closer to home plate and score higher in your work if you come up with innovative ideas—a difficult but effective way to show your higher-level capabilities. In her book *Strategies for Women at Work*, Janice LaRouche tells how she exhibited innovative ideas when, as director of volunteers in a home and hospital for the aged, she created a program that solved a major problem for the institution. The hospital was in the middle of a slum, and the neighborhood kids found the building a likely target for throwing rocks, breaking windows, and assaulting patients and staff on the street.

Although the problem was not her responsibility, Janice decided that the kids might be acting as they did because they were fooled by the seeming wealth of the stainless steel, glass, and marble buildings and had no idea that, if any people were worse off than they were, it was the helpless residents who had little hope of ever getting better. She began to feel that if the kids understood who they were attacking, they would see that their anger had been misdirected.

"My idea was to bring these youngsters into the hospital as volunteers, and, with some maneuvering, I convinced the administration to go along with my efforts," she wrote. "To get the kids interested and involved, I toured them through the buildings and showed them how much help these old and fragile people needed. The youngsters responded with real compassion, pitching in as wheelchair-pushers, recreational aids, and even as assistants to the security guards to prevent the very crimes that they themselves had been committing.

"Because I dealt with the kinds of delicate sociopolitical problems that are central concerns to top management, I began to look like a candidate for higher-level responsibility," Janice LaRouche concluded. "Indeed, soon after, I was offered one of the top jobs in the field."

IDENTIFY POWER STRUCTURES

Unfortunately, such attributes as

- maintaining a good attitude,
- working hard and accumulating knowledge,

- developing top-notch "People Skills,"
- asking for more responsibility,
- managing your time and yourself, and
- coming up with innovative ideas

will not be the only attributes that help you move up on the job. You will also have to make sure you work "smart" and develop a good understanding of how working-world games are played. It is comforting to believe that hard work, skills, and loyalty will get you what you deserve. Even though they are essential, they are not enough. You also need to recognize power structures and politics.

"Every organization has two power structures," reports John Crystal. "One is the visible power structure that's shown on the organization chart. The other is the invisible power structure, made up of some of the movers and shakers not shown on the organization chart. Look at the organization chart and personnel manual for about half an hour. Then sit back and look at the invisible structure that really has the power."

Generally, when you play the complex game of office politics by developing relationships and working through the invisible power structure, you set yourself up for learning the ropes, gleaning important information from the grapevine, advancing on the job, and seeing that office politics work for you.

"Office politics have a lot to do with who gets what, when, and how, and most people see them as a war game between good and evil," believes Marilyn Moats Kennedy, author of *Office Politics* and founder of Career Strategies, a career-planning and consulting firm.

There is no doubt that at times office politics are evil. However, as there is usually no good way to stay out of politics, how can you survive them and avoid getting burned? First, accept the fact that you will always meet rivalry and that everything will not always be fair and square. Then talk to other workers and bring your grievances out in the open. Chances are that as you listen to and learn from other people, you will find other workers are nursing problems similar to yours. This tempers the isolation of going it alone.

If trouble does brew, try to dispel negatives with directness, discretion, and diplomacy. Do not overreact and put your ego on the line at every confrontation, and do not ever criticize people in writing. It could come back to haunt you.

If you are ever set up for failure—say someone "loses" the job assignment that you should be getting—keep a log, documenting your work activities, including the time you receive work assignments or when you do not receive them.

OBTAIN PROMOTIONS AND RAISES

Despite the best skills and dedication, track records are not always rewarded at promotion time. Sometimes you get the promotion without the raise that goes with it. Other times new people come in to do the job you want. It is then that you have to negotiate and ask.

"In my situation promotions came along, but money did not always arrive at the same time," Mary Ann Pope admitted. "Ultimately I had to negotiate with my boss to get into line with what the job was worth. I had to say why I felt I was worth more money. These things are never easy and before I did it I practiced, so I wouldn't sound demanding or defensive."

To prepare for getting more money, keep a record of your duties, responsibilities, skills, and accomplishments. Also, be sure to record how your responsibilities have increased and what you do (or have done) that's over and above your job. Then ask for more than you expect to get as this allows for the give and take that is part of negotiation.

One frequent reaction from a boss is, "Other people are doing good jobs, too, and they're not receiving a raise." When that happens, Sherry Chastain, author of *Winning the Salary Game* advocates looking employers squarely in the eye and saying nothing. "That's their problem, not yours," she notes. "But if you can't handle that tactic say 'I'm only talking about myself.'"

It is possible the subject of degrees will come up, so if an employer says the advancement and money you want are beyond what is generally given to people without a four-year degree, stress experience and accomplishments—as you have done all along. Simultaneously, re-emphasize the fact that you are confident you can perform as well as people with a degree if you are given the chance.

Janice LaRouche says: "Companies are not as enamored of credentials as they sometimes appear to be, even though they may include specific educational requirements in job descriptions. Good managers know that the practical wisdom gained from being steeped in a company and in a job, day in and day out, will usually far surpass what is learned in any school, no matter how prestigious. If you are in this situation, the lack of a credential is not enough reason to turn you down."

CHANGE YOUR JOB OR CAREER WHEN THAT IS THE RIGHT MOVE FOR YOU

In the event your negotiations do not elicit promotions and raises, and there is little chance for advancement where you are or you have been laid off or fired, it is time to consider moving on and transferring your skills and experiences to another job or career. Again, consult your library for helpful books on job changing.

Admittedly, for many people a job change can be traumatic. But with jobs, as with everything else in life, there is a time to come and a time to go, and making a move may win you increased responsibility and money.

John Crystal tells the story of a man who took a job with an automobile manufacturer as soon as he finished high school. He worked primarily with spark plugs, and through the years he managed to rise to a middle-level supervisor's job.

He also acquired a love for art because his wife was a dedicated art teacher. Things were going well for him. He worked with automobiles during the week and spent his weekends at art shows and museums. Then his company decided to move his division to Chicago, and job "experts" the company brought in told all the employees who did not want to move that the only thing that they could do would be to transfer to another auto company. That was easier said than done as all other companies were cutting back, too.

The man analyzed his status and came to the conclusion that the environment in which he would like to spend the rest of his life was the art world. But who would read a résumé stating:

<u>Objective: Art World</u>

Education: High school graduate
Experience: Middle-level supervisor for automobile manufacturer
Specialty: Spark plugs
Interests: Art shows and art museums

"He had to stay away from ordinary procedures and find out something he could do superbly that the art world needed and didn't have," said Crystal. "When he realized that, it didn't take him more than a week to come up with the idea that most people who are crazy about art aren't equally crazy about balancing checkbooks and administrating."

When the man assessed his background, he saw that if there was one thing the automobile company had taught its employees, it was to be very efficient in administration. Consequently, with administration as his goal, he surveyed art institutions and looked for those that needed sharper administration. When he uncovered a need, he settled on three choices where he knew some people from his weekend contacts.

"In each case instead of going to the personnel department where he'd be asked 'Where's your M.F.A.?' he went to the official in charge of administrative efficiency and offered a strong business proposal showing what he could do for the institution," explained Crystal.

"The first institution was interested but turned him down. His second choice—one of the largest art institutions in Manhattan—hired him as office manager at more money than he had been paid by the auto company. And he did so well that a year later he was made vice-president of administration."

In this case the job move did not call for relocation. But we are a mobile society, so it is possible that your next move may mean leaving your area.

"If you're dedicated to moving up you've got to make those commitments," advised Ronald Pilenzo. "But fifty to seventy-five percent of today's job candidates eliminate themselves because they're not prepared to do that. They bring up all kinds of reasons.

"But if you're in New York and there's a job in Rhode Island, you can't rationalize that you won't go because your mother-in-law lives above you in the upstairs apartment. You either have to take your mother-in-law with you—or do something else to go there. You have to make choices and decisions about jobs, and if they're not in your area you may need to widen your circle."

chapter eleven

Parting Advice From Those Who Have Made It

"College certainly isn't for everyone!" emphasized Gary Dinnebeil who, at the age of 31, owns a successful construction company and who, at the time I talked with him, had just finished building a Victorian home priced at $560,000.

"In school I was a C and D student, so I left home right after high school to live on my own and learn to be a carpenter," he said. "I took a few courses at a community college. But my real learning was on the job.

"On my first job, with a carpet laying firm, I cut off the bottoms of doors so they would clear the carpet. Next I spent a couple of years learning from experienced carpenters as I worked on jobs in different aspects of the business. I also read a lot."

At 20, Gary began picking up small repair jobs on his own, and, as more and more work came to him through referrals from customers, he decided to start his own business.

"At first, I built shelves, installed windows, moved doors, and constructed porches and decks," he explained. "Then before I realized it I was being asked to do additions and renovations. By this time I had people working for me, so as soon as I had enough capital, I built my first house on speculation. It was a two-family structure that became one of the first in New Jersey to be sold as a condominium. The price was $203,000 and from that start I went on to building single family homes, that run from $200,000 to $300,000. Some were built on speculation, and some under contract with the owners.

"One of the good things about my work is that with my varied experience, I'm able to be flexible," Dinnebeil said. "When money is tight or the market is slow, I fall back on framing, commercial work, or additions or renovations.

"But I *like* building houses, and I love the challenge of taking a blueprint and making it a reality. The ability to visualize a finished product from a set of drawings is the quality that has helped me most."

Unlike Dinnebeil, who got Cs and Ds, Lisa Rogak did

well in school. But she was bored with classrooms, so instead of staying in college, she became an entrepreneur and the 21-year-old publisher of *Consuming Passions*, a newsletter for women with eating disorders, such as anorexia, bulimia, and compulsive eating.

"You can succeed without a college degree if you *think* you'll succeed," insists Lisa. "But if you feel you're going to work the rest of your life in something you don't want to do because you don't have a degree, you'll be saddled with that idea and be unable to use your abilities to their fullest.

"On the other hand, if you believe that going out into the world without a degree is a challenge that you'd like to meet, fine! In the end, it's mainly your determination that will get you through life, not a piece of paper. When you show initiative that can overshadow your lack of a college degree.

"I was always primed to go to college, so I went to a university for two months mainly to please my mother," she admitted. "But then I dropped out to start a catering service called 'The Pianist Caterer.' I had 12 years of piano training, and I loved to cook, so I decided to combine the two and create a job for myself preparing food and entertaining at parties."

Lisa got her business known through newspaper and radio interviews. But food was her nemesis, because she had already had anorexia and was, then, a bulimia victim. Because of the conflict between her work and food, she gave up her catering service and tried breaking into writing, via articles on eating disorders as she knew the subject so well. To support herself while getting started, she took a part-time job.

"All I got from my work was rejection slips," she conceded, "so one day while wondering where to send my eating disorder pieces next, I got a brainstorm and decided to combine them into a newsletter and sell the newsletter through subscriptions to women with eating problems."

After establishing a format and lining up a printer,

Lisa advertised in other newsletters and obtained newspaper publicity. Later, when her newsletter was mentioned in *Ms* magazine, *Consuming Passions* was "on fire," according to Lisa's description. As she produces it from her Brooklyn home, her circulation grows.

You can get your own work "on fire"—without a college degree—if, like Lisa, you are endowed with initiative and determination, and if you follow this wise advice from non-college people who have made it.

READ!

"In many ways I believe the most important factor in my success professionally and personally is that I read so much and get so much from books and magazines," stressed Barbara Brabec. "Reading is what keeps me psyched up. Reading is what gives me the ideas I use to develop various projects. Reading is what enables me to learn more about the business world.

"When I assumed full responsibility for running a publishing house, I read trade publications, newsletters, marketing books and periodicals, library journals, and books on copywriting, editing, publishing, printing, design, and promotions," she stated, "and after working all day on the job and reading every evening at home, I acquired the probable equivalent of a degree in both journalism and direct marketing."

From every standpoint, reading encourages the lifelong learning that helps you grow personally, vocationally, academically, economically, and socially.

"When I was in school and not necessarily doing well, I read such books as *Think and Grow Rich* and *Grow Rich!—With Peace of Mind* by Napoleon Hill and as I worked toward my goals I had no reason to believe I couldn't do whatever I wanted to do," commented Joe Meister, who cooked up the idea for House of Bread.

"I've always been a voracious reader," added public relations counselor David Mier. "My father invested in stocks as a hobby, so I became interested in business and began to read business publications at a very early age. You have to keep tabs on what is taking place in business and in the world.

"As a child I had an excellent grounding in language," he went on, "and I'm a firm believer that the ability to use the tool of language is important. If you can't read, write, and articulate well you obviate chances to succeed and you can't communicate what you have to offer. A mastery of language helped me take advantage of management opportunities even though I had no college degree."

OPEN YOUR MOUTH AND SPEAK UP

"The worst that can happen when you ask is that someone will say 'No,'" says Mary Ann Pope. "When I felt I had outgrown my temporary employment service job in Newark and learned there was an opening in Philadelphia, I had to say I wanted that branch," she declared.

"Before that I was one of those typical persons waiting for someone to come along and say 'Hey, you're doing a good job. What would you like to have?' But that's not the way things work, and I was forced to speak up one day when our senior vice-president phoned and opened the conversation by asking how I was.

"That day I answered, 'Terrible,' and when she said 'What's wrong?' I told her very frankly that when our company opened a new office in the area where I worked I thought I'd be asked to manage it. Instead it was given to somebody else.

"I'll always remember her answer because she responded, with great surprise, 'But we didn't know you wanted it.' It was then I learned about Philadelphia and when I said I would like that job, I was promoted to it.

"That was a lesson in speaking up and over the years I've said many times that if we don't ask for what we want it isn't that people don't give it to us—we never asked for it."

HAVE DRIVE

"The thing that contributed most to my progress was drive," advises wood care authority, Homer Formby. "Even today I'm never satisfied with sitting still. It's not a money thing. When you have that drive, it keeps pushing you to do other things.

"When I started out I gave myself a good talking to. I asked myself 'Is this what I want to do, because I'm going to have to work myself half to death to get where I want to be.' I decided I was going to make a good life for myself and no one was going to stop me."

"If you have all the education in the world, and all the money backing you, yet you lack the drive and the spirit, you're not going to go very far. Ask yourself if you're willing to work hard enough and sweat enough. Are you willing to work 12–14 hour days? If so, there are opportunities out there."

"The most important advice I would give nondegree people is to have this tremendous drive," emphasizes photographer and college professor Arthur Leipzig. "If you care about your work and have a passion for it, it will overcome a great deal of difficulty."

BUILD A REPUTATION FOR HONESTY, INTEGRITY, AND TRUTH

"There's no substitute for honesty and integrity at any level," comments Joseph Nicolato. "If you've made up your mind that you're not going to get the four-year degree, these traits can make up for the lack of it."

"One of the most important things I've learned is to be truthful," agreed Homer Formby. "The day you start lying is the day you create a monster because you have to tell another lie, and another, and another. Keep your word. Never promise anything unless you know what you're talking about. If you have a problem and can't meet your deadline, call and explain. Disasters happen, and anybody will understand that. But when you start lying to people, it's only going to take a little while to find out and then they'll never trust you."

"From where I stand I'd tell people they should be forthright, honest, and direct," stated Howard Shenson. "They should work on the quality of saying what they mean, and without withholding the truth, do it in a way that's sensitive to other people's needs and feelings."

EXPECT SOME FAILURES AND MISTAKES

Success is even sweeter after you have learned from some failures. For example, if you ask Joe Meister how many unsuccessful businesses he has started he answers, "Only five—and that's not much when you think how many businesses there are.

"I've had some setbacks," he concedes. "But you get your education one way or another, and the thing I've always wanted most is to start something inflation-proof that also performs a service to people. Bread is that. It's not just the 'staff of life.' It *is* life. In ancient Rome, a baker ranked above a senator because the baker held the life of the people literally in his hands."

"Every year I look back and think, 'Boy, did I make mistakes when I was 21, 26, 31 or whatever'," acknowledges David Mier. "But there is value in unbiased retrospect, learning from mistakes, and working at getting better."

Homer Formby adds: "When you make a decision that goes wrong, say 'I made a mistake, and I won't do that again.' Then go on and on."

MAKE SACRIFICES AND TAKE RISKS

Security does not exist in this world. When your goal is a satisfying job that will give you what you want from life, you generally have to pay for it with sacrifice and risk. Be sure to weigh the sacrifice and measure what the cost will be. Then, if the cost is not too high, make reasonable sacrifices.

"Life is an equal opportunity employer," points out Joe Meister. "It will give you what you want. But you always have to pay for it. You have to make sacrifices."

"Whenever you hear somebody say, 'I didn't get that,' it isn't that he didn't get it," Meister continued. "He didn't want to pay the price. He didn't want to sacrifice his time and pleasure. He didn't want to take the chance of losing anything. But if you make necessary sacrifices and take the necessary risks it will pay off eventually.

"A senator referred to me as having qualities like a river boat gambler," declared aviation executive Allen Paulson in an interview in *Leaders* magazine. "I guess he wasn't too far wrong. River boat gamblers take risks. I have taken many risks, but I always try to hedge my risks by thinking ahead and thinking what the dividends would be. Don't put all your eggs in one basket if you are going to take a risk!"

HANG IN AND BE TENACIOUS

"I think what contributed most to my progress was the ability to stick to it," declares guitarist Duncan Cleary. "The music industry is an expecially tough business with a lot of big disappointments and waiting for all kinds of promised work that never really happens.

"But if you have the talent and really want this field you have to take the good with the bad and keep hanging in."

Homer Formby reinforces this advice. "It took me seven years to develop my furniture refinisher, working in my spare time," he explained. "But never once did I say 'I can't do it.' I kept on and on and eventually it paid off."

"Generally, the person most likely to succeed without a four-year degree is prepared to do things the hard way, ready to take hard knocks, and willing to keep coming back," concluded environmentalist Michael Frome.

BE OPEN TO FLEXIBILITY

While being tenacious, you also have to be flexible and sufficiently open-minded to admit that some of your plans do not always work out well. "You'd like them to work, but when they don't you have to ask 'What other avenues can I take?'" advises Mary Ann Pope.

"I don't mean opting for a new route without regard for people or ethics," she was quick to add. "But you have to look at alternatives and say 'This old approach was beneficial once.' But now some things are different and we have to get a new approach.

To this Suzanne Hill, the former singer-turned-businesswoman-and-consultant, adds: "Everything that ever happened in my life was a step in another direction from what I had done before."

LOVE YOUR WORK AND
DO WHAT YOU WANT TO DO

"The one sustaining thing that has always brought me happiness has been my work," says Fay Mitzner, the doll clothes designer. "I absolutely love what I'm doing, and I have never been sorry I didn't get a college degree. Throughout my life I've told my sons, 'Don't ever do something that you don't like—decide what you like and go after it.'"

Madame Wellington of the fake diamonds fame is also known for advising people to do what they love to do. In fact, she tells the story of receiving a phone call late one night in which a male voice told her "I met you 20 years ago, and it's very important that I see you." Later when Madame Wellington met him, he could not wait to tell her "You told me if I didn't like what I was doing to get out. Today I'm worth $16 million.'"

Michael Levine, owner of the fastest growing entertainment public relations firm in Hollywood, has loved his work—and being an entrepreneur—ever since, in high school, he bought blocks of concert tickets and sold them to others at a profit. His interest in concerts went with him to college. Then, when he dropped out at age 18, he became a self-employed concert promoter. In the five years he worked at that, he promoted over 1000 entertainment events.

"I learned by doing," said Levine, who is also author of *The Address Book: How To Reach Anyone Who's Anyone*, which contains an alphabetical listing of 3,500 notables. "In the process I picked up fundamental principles about business. Later, with a small savings, my wife and I moved to California and started a television guide called *TV News*.

Because Levine was endowed with common sense, a knowledge of business basics, and an instinct for putting a magazine together, the magazine was successful, and he and his wife kept it going till he sold it after seven years.

Next Levine went to work in the television department of the country's largest entertainment public relations firm. While there, he handled special projects for Kenny Rogers, Henry Fonda, and Hugh Hefner (among others) until he left to form a small personalized firm. Again, he took business basics with him and Hollywood starmaker, Jay Bernstein, has labeled Michael Levine "the best young publicist in town." In 1980 when he was appointed by Governor Jerry Brown to the seven-member California Governor's Advisory Board, he was the youngest person ever appointed to that statewide post.

EXCEL AT WHAT YOU CHOOSE TO DO

Along with liking what you do, another important ingredient is a strong desire to excel at your work and do it better than anybody else.

"When Bud Wilkinson, who coached the University of Oklahoma's football team for 40 consecutive wins, was asked what he looked for in his players he answered 'There's no substitute for talent.'" recalled Joseph Nicolato. "But then Wilkinson added, 'If you have 100 percent talent and 20 percent desire you are only applying that talent 20 percent of the time. What I look for is that rare combination of ingredients between talent and desire. Let's say the talent is 80 percent but the desire is 100 percent. Now I'm getting 80 percent talent 100 percent of the time.'

"This is what I tell my people. This is the drummer to march by."

MAKE EVERY EXPERIENCE COUNT

"Every ounce of work experience has formed the foundation for all that I'm doing today," points out Barbara Brabec. "That includes my teen years in a corn canning factory where I had to cut worms off ears of corn, chopping at them with a big knife. The corn splattered all over me, and every hour it had to be scraped off my face and rubber apron.

"What I learned here was discipline. I was working to earn money to buy a marimba, so I was willing to do almost anything to get it—even this kind of awful job. The cans rolling along a conveyor line made a terrible racket. It was enough to drive people nuts, but I learned how to shut out the noise by thinking about interesting things. To this day, there is no noise that can stop me from working. I'm able to pull down an invisible blind and keep out anything I don't want to get through. This enables me to work productively even when the atmosphere is negative, so the corn canning factory had its value."

Today Sandra Dartus has an enviable job as project coordinator and director of marketing for the Jackson Brewery development in the French Quarter of New Orleans. Her rise to this top level professional job began in her last year in high school, when she started making experience count under a Cooperative Office Education Program.

"The day after I graduated, I started working full time as a receptionist in the school board office," she said. "A few months later I was transferred from the receptionist desk to the secretarial pool, and in that job I served as a backup for the secretary to the superintendent."

Within four years, Sandra became secretary to the superintendent. At the time, however, the salary scale for the school board was separated into two categories—professional and nonprofessional—and without the benefit of a college degree, there was little opportunity for Sandra to advance either financially or by title. During the eight years she worked at the job, her workload and job responsibilities were equal to that of the professional staff. But there was no category in which she could fit, and because of "rocking the educational boat" she could not receive recognition.

"At the superintendent's insistence I enrolled in a community college and took a varied combination of courses," explained Sandra. "While I was taking courses, however, the superintendent retired, and when an outsider was appointed to follow him my position seemed somewhat tenuous, so I sought other employment.

"My next job was with a sulphur company, but the job was extremely boring, so after three months I moved to a spot as administrative assistant to the two principals of Berger & Burrus Investments. I was still taking courses at the community college, but the increasing demands of my job necessitated my dropping out of school. Then a few months after I began working with Berger & Burrus, they acquired the Jackson Brewery property."

This move was a good one for Sandra because she soon became heavily involved in the renovation of the old Jax Brewhouse and the planning for the specialty stores, restaurants, and food and beverage bars to be housed in the restoration.

"Before too long the rapid growth of the company made it virtually impossible for me to continue working as administrative assistant to both Mr. Burrus and Mr. Berger," she declared, "so, because of the time constraints of the Brewery development, I was promoted to project coordinator. I also continued to function as Mr. Berger's administrative assistant."

One of Sandra's major accomplishments as project coordinator was the planning of a "Celebration of JAX" party. Because this was such a large endeavor, the need for an in-house marketing person was often brought up and when the event was highly successful—and a personal success for Sandra—her work as project director put her in line as the main candidate for the in-house marketing job. Consequently, she became both project coordinator and director of marketing.

REMEMBER TO MAKE YOURSELF VISIBLE

"You're a salesperson selling yourself," maintains Lisa Rogak, "so know your good points and be aggressive and enthusiastic. Then you'll be noticed for *that*, not for the piece of paper you don't have."

Sharon Morgan, the "intrapreneur" in advertising and public relations, also believes in letting people know what you are doing. "But not in an offensive way," she hastens to add. "You can't walk around saying 'Look what I did. Look how good I am.' You need more subtle visibility."

"Public relations is fifty percent doing the job and fifty percent telling people you've done it," says Michael Levine. "But *everybody* can have a public relations campaign because public relations is more than that. It's also the firmness of a handshake. The sincerity of a smile. A thank-you note. A birthday card. These are things all of us can do for visibility."

REFUSE TO BE THREATENED BY NOT HAVING A DEGREE

Unfortunately, some people feel second class when they do not have a four-year degree, as illustrated by one well-spoken man, whose self-education and outstanding contribution to his community, family, and work exceeds the attainments of many others in his business and social circles.

"But I still feel like the low man on the totem pole whenever I'm with people who know I haven't been to college," he confessed. "Just to give you an example, I went to a party the other night and when two people who were talking to me mentioned fraternities and college I made an excuse to leave and go home rather than have to admit that I hadn't been to college."

"A lot of people will try to make you feel that a degree is the most important thing in the world and that there's a personal or social stigma in not having one," warns Duncan Cleary. "There have been instances when I've been sure someone was trying to make me feel inferior because of this.

"To be perfectly honest this has bothered me at times since some people seem to assume automatically that you're not as intelligent as they when you lack the degree. But I no longer get hung up on that because the good life for me is being able to make a living doing what I love the most. When you face up to that, the degree doesn't make any difference."

ENGRAVE "I CAN" IN YOUR HEART AND MIND

"One thing I always tell students today—I teach at the Fashion Institute of Technology—is not to be discouraged," stated designer Calvin Klein in an article in *Parade* magazine. "You have to want it, and if you really want it enough, you can, I honestly believe, achieve anything you want. To this day, I'm still a positive thinker. I think you have to make an enormous commitment to your work. You have to put that in front of a lot of other things."

"So often people automatically say 'You don't have the training—you can't do that,'" Suzanne Hill declared. "Well, my friends and I who have done what we wanted all agree that if we got an award in which we thanked the producers, directors, parents, children, boy next door, et cetera, we'd say 'This is a tribute to all the people who told us 'You can't.' Now we're saying 'We did.'"

"If people say you can't do it, that's garbage," added John Crystal. "All you have to do is learn how."

"A lot of people told me I wouldn't be able to do what I wanted in the music field," said Duncan Cleary. "But if you feel strongly enough about it who is to say you can't."

"You simply don't listen to the people who tell you you can't," concluded Joe Meister. "Whatever you want to be—whatever you want to do—you act it, feel it, believe it."

HAVE UNSHAKABLE FAITH IN YOUR ABILITIES

In a keynote address to the Society of Craft Designers, Barbara Brabec said: "Your success in business is the result of your intense belief that you will succeed—and it is not dependent upon superior brainpower nor even experience. Indeed it isn't important that you know little about something when you start. It's only important that you learn as you go along.

"When the publisher for whom I worked was among the victims of the ill-fated flight that crashed at O'Hare in 1979 I was the only person left in the book division besides an order and shipping clerk which is how I became a publisher and general manager. The company was a small one and my book *Creative Cash* was the first book in its line. Anyone could see that if I didn't finish the job the publisher started it would never get done, so I volunteered to do it.

"It was the greatest challenge of my business life, and the thing I was really counting on to get me through was an unshakable faith in my own abilities and an intense belief that I could do it, even without a college degree."

"I've always believed that what puts you where you want to go is yourself—that drive you have in your mind, in your heart, in your soul and in your being," says Homer Formby. "You say to yourself 'I'm going to do it' and you don't let anything stand in your way."

"I've seen a lot of people without an education who

have excellent jobs because they wanted to be the best in what they do. I know one man who at one time had several hundred incorporations under his name. I believe he left school after the 6th grade. He's a very wealthy man and is still going strong. And the man who helped me establish Formby's didn't have a college degree."

LIVE BY YOUR OWN DEFINITION OF SUCCESS

Success is so highly personal we must all define it on our own. Most of the non-college people who discussed it for this book feel it is doing what you want to do in the best way you know how.

"It's having a job or career that makes it a pleasure to go to work every day, that gives you something to look forward to for the following day, that provides ample room for growth in the future and that supplies you with enough income to keep you from worrying about your primal needs," maintains Gerald Kern. "Ideally, it is also nice if what you do for a living is perceived as useful to your fellow human beings."

Other people have defined success as:

- "Accomplishing and learning something every day that benefits you and others."
- "Reaching the goals you set for yourself."
- "Using all of your talents and feeling valued and challenged."
- "Gaining respect and recognition for your work from your contemporaries, family, and friends."
- "Attaining personal happiness, personal satisfaction, personal self-esteem."
- "Striking the right balance between job success and personal success."

"For business success, I'm goal oriented and I like to achieve," said Mary Ann Pope. "But when it comes to personal success, I'd say that what's successful there is loving people and having them love you back."

Without this kind of personal success, job success means little and the cost is very large.

"I asked for a successful career, and I got it," reported one top achiever. "But I got it at a high cost. I forgot to prioritize love and relationships and put them on the list of things to do. I forgot to put laughter on and I also forgot about fun. I pushed these things out of my mind to have an affair with work.

"You can have a fixation on your work, and certainly there's a great correlation between fixation and success. But at what cost? All the trappings of success can be completely meaningless without personal success."

Money alone can be meaningless, too, if your only goal in obtaining it is money for money's sake.

"My definition of a successful life has very little to do with a lot of money," stated Barbara Brabec. "When someone in Illinois won a 40 million dollar lottery I was asked 'What would you do if you'd won it?' My answer had to be 'If I were to win a lottery I couldn't stop working just because I had money!'

"I wouldn't want to give up the business I've worked so hard to develop, and I can readily understand why millionaires who could take it easy often keep on with their work. They work to contribute something to living."

The idea of making a contribution continued to come up innumerable times as I talked to people about their success.

"When I was the keynote speaker at Natural Resources Day at Colorado State University, I was on a panel with others telling how we became successful," summed up Michael Frome. "That made me think about it, and I have come to the conclusion that success has to happen every day. It has to happen tomorrow, so it's more of an open-ended challenge than a closed book. The great use of a life is creating something that outlasts it."

In the final analysis, we all use our lives in different ways and—with or without a college degree—that is as it should be.

And, as so many others have shown, you *can* succeed

without a degree if, rather than thinking of what you *can't* do, you concentrate on what you *can* do and go for it all the way.

Your life is what you make it yourself.

So ask for—and get—the best!

RESOURCE DIRECTORY

BOOKS FOR FURTHER INFORMATION

A Woman's Book of Money: A Guide to Financial Independence, by Sylvia Auerbach, Dolphin Books, Garden City, NY.

A Woman's Guide to Starting a Business, by Claudia Jessup and Genie Chipps, Holt, Rinehart and Winston, New York, NY.

Arts & Crafts Market, Writers Digest, Cincinnati, OH.

Be Your Own Boss: A Woman's Guide to Planning and Running Her Business, by Barbara S. McCaslin and Patricia McNamara, Prentice-Hall, Inc., Englewood Cliffs, NJ.

Blue Collar Jobs for Women, by Muriel Lederer, E. P. Dutton & Co., Inc., New York, NY.

By Hand: A Guide to Schools and Careers in Crafts, by Tom Hebert and John Coyne, E. P. Dutton & Co., Inc., New York, NY.

Career Opportunities in Crafts, by Elyse Sommer, Crown Publishers, Inc., New York, NY.

Career Planning and Job Hunting for Today's Student: The Nonjob Interview Approach, by Edmond Billingsley, Goodyear Publishing Company, Inc., Santa Monica, CA.

Choices and Changes: A Career Book for Men, by Joyce Slayton Mitchell, The College Board, New York, NY.

Choosing to Work: An Action-Orientated Job Finding Book, by Leonard Cohen, Reston Publishing Co., Reston, VA.

Creative Cash: How to Sell Your Crafts, Needlework, Designs and Know-How, by Barbara Brabec, Barbara Brabec Productions, Naperville, IL.

Discover What You're Best At: The National Career Aptitude Test, by Barry Gale and Linda Gale, Simon & Schuster, New York, NY.

Education and Jobs: The Great Training Robbery, by I. Berg, Praeger Publishers, Inc., New York, NY.

Free Publicity - A Step-by-Step Guide, by Dave Knesel, Sterling Publishing Co., Inc., New York, NY.

Free Time - Making Your Leisure Count, by Jan Gault, John Wiley & Sons, Inc., New York, NY.

From Kitchen to Career, by Shirley Sloan Fader, Stein and Day, Briarcliff Manor, NY

Getting a Better Job, by David Gootnick, McGraw-Hill Book Company, New York, NY.

Get It All Done and Still Be Human, by Robbie and Tony Fanning, Chilton Book Company, Radnor, PA.

Getting Skilled: A Guide to Private Trade and Technical Schools, by Tom Hebert and John Coyne, E. P. Dutton & Co., Inc., New York, NY.

Get the Best of Yourself! by Katherine Nash, Grosset and Dunlap, Inc., New York, NY.

Getting Things Done: The ABCs of Time Management, by Edwin C. Bliss, Charles Scribner's Sons, New York, NY.

Go Hire Yourself an Employer, by Richard K. Irish, Doubleday & Co., Inc., New York, NY.

Homemade Money, by Barbara Brabec, Betterway Publications, White Hall, VA.

How to Earn More Money From Your Crafts, by Merle Dowd, Doubleday & Co., Inc., New York, NY.

How Mail-Order Fortunes Are Made: Everything You Need to Know About Mail Order, by Alfred Stern, Arco Publishing Co., Inc., New York, NY.

How to Beat the Employment Game, David Noer, Ten Speed Press, Berkeley, CA.

How to Develop Self-Confidence & Influence People by Public Speaking, by Dale Carnegie, Pocket Books, New York, NY.

How to Establish and Operate Your Own Consulting Practice, by Howard Shenson, Prentice-Hall, Inc., Englewood Cliffs, NJ.

How to Make a Habit of Success, by Bernard Haldane, Acropolis Books, Washington, DC.

How to Make Money with Your Crafts, by Leta W. Clark, William Morrow & Co., Inc., New York, NY.

How to Open Your Own Shop or Gallery, by Leta W. Clark, St. Martin's Press, New York, NY.

How to Organize and Operate a Small Business, by Clifford M. Baumback, Kenneth Lawyer, and Pearce C. Kelley, Prentice-Hall, Inc., Englewood Cliffs, NJ.

How to Pick the Right Small Business Opportunity: The Key to Success in Your Business, by Kenneth J. Albert, McGraw-Hill Book Company, New York, NY.

How to Run a Small Business, by J. K. Lasser, McGraw-Hill Book Company, New York, NY.

Franchising - How to Select a Business of Your Own, by Robert Nietz, Hawthorn Books, Inc., New York.

How to Sell Your Arts and Crafts, by Loretta Holz, Charles Scribner's Sons, New York, NY.

How to Sell Your Artwork: A Complete Guide for Commercial and Fine Artists, by Milton K. Berlye, Prentice-Hall, Inc., Englewood Cliffs, NJ.

How to Start and Manage Your Own Business, by Gardiner G. Greene, The New American Library, Inc., New York, NY.

How to Start and Operate a Mail Order Business, by Julian L. Simon, McGraw-Hill Book Company, New York, NY.

How to Succeed as an Independent Consultant, by Herman Holtz, John Wiley & Sons, Inc., New York, NY.

How to Win in a Job Interview, by Jason Robertson, Prentice-Hall, Inc., Englewood Cliffs, NJ.

How to Write and Use Simple Press Releases That Work, by Kate Kelly, Visibility Enterprises, New York, NY.

Human Relations and Your Career: A Guide to Interpersonal Skills, by David W. Johnson, Prentice-Hall, Inc., Englewood Cliffs, NJ.

I Can Be Anything: A Career Book for Women, by Joyce Slayton Mitchell, The College Board, New York, NY.

Inc. Yourself: How to Profit by Setting Up Your Own Corporation, by Judith H. McQuown, Warner Books, New York, NY.

Jobs: How People Create Their Own, by William C. Ronco, Beacon Press, Boston, MA.

Jobs for Weekends, by Roberta Roesch, Berkley Publishing Corporation, New York, NY.

Job Power Now! The Young People's Job Finding Guide, by Bernard Haldane, Jean Haldane and Lowell Martin, Acropolis Books Ltd., Washington, DC.

Mail Order Know-How, by Cecil C. Hope, Sr., Ten Speed Press, Berkeley, CA.

Mail Order Moonlighting, by Cecil C. Hope, Sr., Ten Speed Press, Berkeley, CA.

Making Vocational Choices: A Theory of Careers, by John L. Holland, Prentice-Hall, Inc., Englewood Cliffs, NJ.

Mary Kay, by Mary Kay Ash, Harper & Row Publishers, Inc., New York, NY.

Mary Kay on People Management, by Mary Kay Ash, Warner Books, New York, NY.

Merchandising Your Job Talents, U.S. Government Printing Office, Washington, DC.

Only In America Opportunity Still Knocks, Horatio Alger Association, Inc., New York, NY.

On Your Own: 99 Alternatives to a 9 to 5 Job, by Kathy Matthews, Vintage Books, New York, NY.

Overeducation in the U.S. Labor Market, by R. W. Rumberger, Praeger Publishers, Inc., New York, NY.

Profits at Your Doorstep, by Judith Weber and Karol White, Hawthorn Books, Inc., New York, NY.

Running Your Own Business, by Howard H. Stern, Crown Publishers, Inc., New York, NY.

Running Your Own Show, by Richard T. Curtin, John Wiley & Sons, Inc., New York, NY.

Skills for Success: A Guide to the Top, by Adele M. Scheele, Ph.D., William Morrow and Company, Inc., New York, NY.

Small Business Management Fundamentals, by Dan Steinhoff, McGraw-Hill Book Company, New York, NY.

Starting and Succeeding in Your Own Small Business, by L. L. Allen, Grosset & Dunlap Inc., New York, NY.

Successful Small Business Management, by Leon Wortman, American Management Association, New York, NY.

The Case Against College, by Caroline Bird, David McKay and Co., New York, NY.

The Complete Job Search Handbook: Presenting the Skills You Need to Get Any Job, and Have a Good Time Doing It, by Howard E. Figler, Holt, Rinehart and Winston, New York, NY.

The Crafts Business Encyclopedia, by Michael Scott, Harcourt Brace Jovanovich, Inc., New York, NY.

The Entrepreneur's Manual, by Richard M. White, Jr., Chilton Book Company, Radnor, PA.

Resource Directory

The Guide to Career Education, by Muriel Lederer, Quadrangle/ The New York Time Book Company, Inc., New York, NY.

The Hidden Job Market, A System to Beat the System, by Tom Jackson, and Davidyne Mayleas, Quadrangle/ The New York Times Book Co., New York, NY.

The Magic of Believing, by Claude Bristol, Pocket Books, New York, NY.

The Professional Photographer - Developing a Successful Career, by Larry Goldman, Doubleday & Co., Inc., New York, NY.

The Publicity Manual, by Kate Kelly, Visibility Enterprises, New York, NY.

The Quick and Easy Way to Effective Speaking, by Dale Carnegie, Pocket Books, New York, NY.

The Quick Job-Hunting Map: A Fast Way to Help, by Richard N. Bolles, Ten Speed Press, Berkeley, CA.

The Three Boxes of Life and How to Get Out of Them, by Richard N. Bolles, Ten Speed Press, Berkeley, CA.

The Work Book, A Guide to Skilled Jobs, by Joyce Slayton Mitchell, Bantam Books, Inc., New York, NY.

There's Always a Right Job for Every Woman, by Roberta Roesch, Perigee, New York, NY.

This Way Out: A Guide to Alternatives to Higher Education, by Tom Hebert, and John Coyne, E. P. Dutton & Co., Inc., New York, NY.

28 Days to a Better Job, by Tom Jackson, Hawthorn Books, Inc., NY.

Welcome to the Real World: A Guide to Making Your First Personal, Financial, and Career Decisions, by Annie Moldafsky, Doubleday & Co., Inc., New York, NY.

What Color Is Your Parachute?, by Richard N. Bolles, Ten Speed Press, Berkeley, CA.

Where Do I Go From Here With My Life?, by John C. Crystal and Richard N. Bolles, Ten Speed Press, Berkeley, CA.

Who's Hiring Who, by Richard Lathrop, Ten Speed Press, Berkeley, CA.

Women's Work Book, by Karin Abarbanel, and Gonnie McClung Siegel, Praeger Publishers, Inc., New York, NY.

Working for Yourself, by Geoff Hewitt, Rodale Press, Emmaus, PA.

You, Inc., by Peter Weaver, Doubleday & Co., Inc., New York, NY.

Your Career: How to Plan It, How to Manage It, How to Change It, by Richard H. Buskirk, The New American Library, Inc., New York, NY.

Your Job-Where to Find It, How to Get It, by Leonard Corwen, Arco Publishing Co., Inc., New York, NY.

Your Résumé - Key to a Better Job, by Leonard Corwen, Arco Publishing Co., Inc., New York, NY.

DIRECTORY OF ORGANIZATIONS AND ASSOCIATIONS

You can write to the following organizations for further information or pamphlets that give, (1) general job information, (2) what people do in each job, (3) qualifications needed for jobs, (4) potential places of employment, (5) working conditions, and (6) training requirements.

All of the addresses provided in this Resource Directory are correct at press time. However, organizations and associations occasionally move and have a change of address. If they leave a forwarding order your mail will be forwarded to them.

Skilled Trades and Crafts

National Roofing Contractors Association
1515 North Harlem Avenue
Oak Park, IL 60302

Association of Home Appliance Manufacturers
20 North Wacker Drive
Chicago, IL 60606

National Association of Plumbing & Heating Contractors
1016 20th Street, N.W.
Washington, DC 20036

International Association of Wall and Ceiling Contractors
1775 Church Street, N.W.
Washington, DC 20036

International Council for Lathing & Plastering
221 No. LaSalle Street
Chicago, IL 60601

Painting and Decorating Contractors Association of America
7223 Lee Highway
Falls Church, VA 22046

National Electrical Contractors Association
1730 Rhode Island N.W.
Washington, DC 20036

National Association of Auto Trim Shops
129 Broadway
Lynbrook, NY 11563

International Association of Firefighters
905 16th Street, N.W.
Washington, DC 20006

National Tooling and Machining Association
9300 Livingston Road
Ft. Washington, MD 20744

Piano Technicians Guild Inc.
P.O. Box 1813
Seattle, WA 98111

National Association of Metal Finishers
248 Lorraine Avenue
Upper Montclair, NJ 07043

Sheet Metal Workers International Association
1000 Connecticut Avenue, N.W.
Washington, DC 20036

American Trucking Association
1616 P Street, N.W.
Washington, DC 20036

Associated Locksmiths of America
11 Elmendorf Street
Kingston, NY 12401

American Foundrymen's Society
Golf and Wolf Roads
Des Plaines, IL 60016

Forging Industry Association
55 Public Square
Cleveland, OH 44113

International Association of Machinists
  and Aerospace Workers
1300 Connecticut Avenue, N.W.
Washington, DC 20036

Plumbing-Heating-Cooling Information Center
35 East Wacker Drive
Chicago, IL 60601

Master Photo Dealers and Finishers Association
603 Lansing Avenue
Jackson, MI 49202

National Terrazzo & Mosaic Association, Inc.
716 Church Street
Alexandria, VA 22314

Air Conditioning and Refrigeration Contractors
  of America
20 North Wacker Drive, Suite 2232
Chicago, IL 60606

Sheet-Metal and Air Conditioning Contractors'
National Association, Inc.
8224 Old Courthouse Road
Tyson's Corner, Vienna, VA 22180

Mechanical Contractors Association of America
666 3rd Avenue, Suite 1464
New York, NY 10017

American Association of Nurserymen, Inc.
835 Southern Building
Washington, DC 20005

Associated General Contractors of America Inc.
1957 E. Street, N.W.
Washington, DC 20006

National Machine Tool Builders Association
2139 Wisconsin Avenue, N.W.
Washington, DC 20007

Tile Contractors Association of America, Inc.
112 North Alfred Street
Alexandria, VA 22314

Brick Institute of America
1750 Old Meadow Road
McLean, VA 22102

American Watchmakers Institute
Box 11011
Cincinnati, OH 45211

The Glamour Industries: Art, Creative Crafts, Communication, Entertainment

Society of American Florist and
   Ornamental Horticulturists
901 N. Washington Street
Alexandria, VA 22314

American Crafts Council
401 Park Avenue, South
New York, NY 10016

Industrial Designers Society of America
1750 Old Meadow Road
McLean, VA 22101

American Educational Theatre Association
1317 F Street, N.W.
Washington, DC 20004

Professional Photographers of America, Inc.
1090 Executive Way
Des Plaines, IL 60018

National Cartoonists Society
9 Ebony Court
Brooklyn, NY 11229

Education Council of the Graphic Arts, Inc.
4615 Forbes Avenue
Pittsburgh, PA 15213

The Newspaper Comics Council, Inc.
Ward Castle, Comly Avenue
Port Chester, NY 10573

Public Relations Society of America Inc.
845 Third Avenue
New York, NY 10022

The American Ceramic Society
4055 North High Street
Columbus, OH 43214

National Association of Schools of Music
One Dupont Circle, N.W.
Washington, DC 20036

National Association of Broadcasters
1771 N Street, N.W.
Washington, DC 20036

Gemological Institute of America
1660 Stewart Street
Santa Monica, CA 90406

National Society of Interior Designers, Inc.
312 East 62nd Street
New York, NY 10021

National Art Education Association
1916 Association Drive
Reston, VA 22091

Business

National Association of Underwriters
1922 F Street, N.W.
Washington, DC 20006

Institute of Life Insurance
277 Park Avenue
New York, NY 10017

National Association of Insurance Women
1847 East 15th Street
Tulsa, OK 74104

The American Society of Travel Agents, Inc.
3 East 54th Street
New York, NY 10022

National Association of Accountants
919 Third Avenue
New York, NY 10022

National Alliance of Homebased Businesswomen
P.O. Box 95
Norwood, NJ 07648

American Bankers Association
1120 Connecticut Avenue, N.W.
Washington, DC 20036

Manufacturers' Agents National Association
P.O. Box 16878
Irvine, CA 92713

Security Industry Association
20 Broad Street
New York, NY 10005

The Society of American Florists
901 North Washington Street
Alexandria, VA 22314

American Association of Advertising Agencies
666 Third Avenue, 13th Floor
New York, NY 10017

National Association of Barber Schools, Inc.
304 South 11th Street
Lincoln, NE 68508

National Barber Styling Career Center
3839 White Plains Road
Bronx, NY 10467

American Bankers Association
Personnel Division
1120 Connecticut Avenue, N.W.
Washington, DC 20036

American Council of Life Insurance
1850 K Street, N.W.
Washington, DC 20006

Sales

National Association of Wholesaler-Distributors
1725 K Street, N.W.
Washington, DC 20006

Sales and Marketing Executives - International
Career Education Department
330 West 42nd Street
New York, NY 10036

National Automobile Dealers
2000 K Street, N.W.
Washington, DC 20006

The National Retail Merchants Association
100 West 31st Street
New York, NY 10001

National Association of Realtors
430 North Michigan Avenue
Chicago, IL 60611

The Direct Mail Marketing Association
6 East 43rd Street
New York, NY 10017

Direct Selling Education Foundation
1730 M Street, N.W., Suite 605
Washington, DC 20036

National Mail Order Association
5818 Venice Boulevard
Los Angeles, CA 90019

National Association of Securities Dealers
1735 K Street, N.W.
Washington, DC 20006

Clerical and Secretarial Work

Professional Secretaries International
2440 Pershing Road
Crown Center G10
Kansas City, MO 64108

The National Task Force on the
 Image of the Secretary
1730 M Street, N.W., Suite 600
Washington, DC 20036

The National Association of
 Legal Secretaries
3005 East Skelly Drive, Suite 120
Tulsa, OK 74105-6397

National Shorthand Reporters Association
118 Park Street, S.E.
Vienna, VA 22180

Computer-Related Jobs

Data Processing Management Association
505 Busse Highway
Park Ridge, IL 60068

Association for Computing Machinery
1133 Avenue of the Americas
New York, NY 10036

American Federation of Information
 Processing Societies, Inc.
1815 North Lynn Street, Suite 800
Arlington, VA 22209

Paraprofessional Careers

The American Society of Radiologic Technologists
645 North Michigan Avenue
Chicago, IL 60611

Society of American Foresters
Wild Acres
5400 Grosvenor Lane
Bethesda, MD 20814.

American Association of Medical Assistants
1 East Wacker Drive, Suite 1510
Chicago, IL 60601

National Commission on Certification of
 Physician's Assistants, Inc.
3384 Peachtree Road, N.E., Suite 560
Atlanta, GA 30326

National Association of Social Workers
1425 H Street, N.W.
Southern Building, Suite 600
Washington, DC 20005

Council on Social Work Education
345 East 46th Street
New York, NY 10017

Resource Directory

American Library Association
50 East Huron Street
Chicago, IL 60611

American Bar Association
Special Committee on Legal Assistants
1155 East 60th Street
Chicago, IL 60637

National Association of Legal Assistants, Inc.
3005 East Skelley Drive, Suite 122
Tulsa, OK 74105

National Federation of Paralegal Associations, Inc.
Ben Franklin Station, P.O. Box 14103
Washington, DC 20044

(NOTE: See listings under "Health" for additional sources.)

Health

American Medical Records Association
John Hancock Center, Suite 1850
875 No. Michigan Avenue
Chicago, IL 60611

National Association for Licensed
  Practical Nurses
10801 Pear Tree Lane
St. Louis, MO 63074

American Dental Association
211 East Chicago Avenue
Chicago, IL 60611

American Dance Therapy Association
2000 Century Plaza, Suite 230
Columbia, MD 21044

American Association for Respiratory
  Therapy
7411 Hines Place
Dallas, TX 75235

National League for Nursing
10 Columbus Circle
New York, NY 10019

American Medical Association
Department of Allied Health Evaluation
535 North Dearborn Street
Chicago, IL 60601

American Hospital Association
840 North Lake Shore Drive
Chicago, IL 60611

American Occupational Therapy Association
6000 Executive Boulevard
Rockville, MD 20852

American Physical Therapy Association
1111 North Fairfax Street
Alexandria, VA 22314

National Therapeutic Recreation Society
1601 North Kent Street
Arlington, VA 22209

American Nurses' Association
2420 Pershing Road
Kansas City, MO 64108

American Art Therapy Association
P.O. Box 11604
Pittsburgh, PA 15228

National Health Council, Inc.
70 West 40th Street
New York, NY 10018

American Industrial Hygiene Association
66 S. Miller Road
Akron, OH 44313

American Society of Safety Engineers
850 Busse Highway
Park Ridge, IL 60068

National Institute for Occupational
  Safety and Health
Division of Training and Manpower
Robert A. Taft Laboratories
4676 Columbia Parkway
Cincinnati, OH 45226

American Association for Health
  Physical Education and Recreation Assoc.
1201 16th Street, N.W.
Washington, DC 20036

National Registry of Emergency Medical
  Technicians
1395 East Dublin-Granville Road
P.O. Box 29233
Columbus, OH 43229

National Society for Histotechnology
5900 Princess Garden Parkway, Suite 805
P.O. Box 36
Lanham, MD 20706

American Society of Cytology
130 South 9th Street, Suite 810
Philadelphia, PA 19107

American Registry of Diagnostic Medical
  Sonography
2810 Burnett, Suite 2N
Cincinnati, OH 45219

National Association for Music Therapy, Inc.
P.O. Box 610
Lawrence, KS 66044

American Medical Technologists
710 Higgins Road
Park Ridge, IL 60068

American Registry of Radiologic
  Technologists
2600 Wayzata Boulevard
Minneapolis, MN 20007

Association of Surgical Technologists, Inc.
8307 Shaffer Parkway
Caller No. E
Littleton, CO 80120

American Academy of Physician's Associates
2150 Pennsylvania Avenue, Room 356
Washington, DC 20037

American Dental Hygienists' Association
444 North Michigan Avenue, Suite 3400
Chicago, IL 60611

Dental Laboratory Technology
National Association of Dental Laboratories
3801 Mt. Vernon Avenue
Alexandria, VA 22305

American Dental Assistants Association
666 North Lake Shore Drive, Suite 1130
Chicago, IL 60611

Technical Jobs

Electronics Industries Association
2001 Eye Street, N.W.
Washington, DC 20006

American Electronics Association
2680 Hanover Street
Palo Alto, CA 94304

Electronics Technicians Association International,
R. R. 3, Box 564
Greencastle, IN 46135

International Society of Certified
    Electronics Technicians
2708 W. Berry Street
Ft. Worth, TX 76109

National Automatic Sprinkler and Fire
  Control Association
P.O. Box 719
Mt. Kisco, NY 10549

American Society for Horticultural Science
National Center for American Horticulture
Mt. Vernon, VA 22121

American Geological Institute
5205 Leesburg Pike
Falls Church, VA 22041

International Federation of Professional
  and Technical Engineers
1126 16th Street, N.W.
Washington, DC 20036

American Society of Heating, Refrigeration
  and Air Conditioning Engineers
1016 20th Street, N.W.
Washington, DC 20036

American Institute of Aeronautics
  and Astronautics
1290 Avenue of the Americas
New York, NY 10104

Academy of Aeronautics
LaGuardia Airport
Flushing, NY 11371

National Electrical Contractors
  Association
1730 Rhode Island, N.W.
Washington, DC 20036

American Optometric Association
7000 Chippewa Street
St. Louis, MO 63119

Associated Opticians of America
1250 Connecticut Avenue, N.W.
Washington, DC 20036

American Society for Quality Control
161 West Wisconsin Avenue
Milwaukee, WI 53203

Society for Technical Communications Inc.
1010 Vermont Avenue, N.W., Suite 421
Washington, DC 20005

National Alliance of TV and
  Electronic Service Association
5908 So. Troy Street
Chicago, IL 60629

Institute for the Certification of
  Engineering Technicians
2029 K Street, N.W.
Washington, DC 20006

Refrigeration Service Engineers Society
2720 Des Plaines Avenue
Des Plaines, IL 60018

The Society of Automotive Engineers, Inc.
400 Commonwealth Drive
Warrendale, PA 15096

American Institute for Design and Drafting
3119 Price Rd.
Bartlesville, OK 74003

Farm and Industrial Equipment Institute
650 Wrigley Building N
Chicago, IL 60611

Water Pollution Control Federation
3900 Wisconsin Avenue
Washington, DC 20016

National Electric Sign Association
600 Hunter Drive
Oak Brook, IL 60521

Service Occupations

National Beauty Career Center
3839 White Plains Road
Bronx, NY 10467

Culinary Institute of America
Box 53
Hyde Park, NY 12538

National Institute for the Foodservice Industry
20 North Wacker Drive, Suite 2620
Chicago, IL 60606

Council on Hotel, Restaurant, and
  Institutional Education
1522 K Street, N.W.
Washington, DC 20005

Educational Institute of the American Hotel
  and Motel Association
1407 South Harrison Road
East Lansing, MI 48823

The American Hotel and Motel Association
888 Seventh Avenue
New York, NY 10019

National Council for Homemaker-Home
  Health Aide Services
67 Irving Place - 6th Floor
New York, NY 10003

American Meat Institute
59 East Van Buren
Chicago, IL 60605

Automotive Service Industry Association
230 North Michigan Avenue
Chicago, IL 60601

Automotive Service Council
4001 Warren Boulevard
Hillside, IL 60162

National Industrial Recreation Association
20 North Wacker Drive
Chicago, IL 60606

National Committee on Household
 Employment
1625 I Street, N.W.
Washington, DC 20006

National Funeral Directors Association
135 West Wells Street
Milwaukee, WI 53203

National Foundation of Funeral Services
1614 Central Street
Evanston, IL 60201

Transportation

Association of American Railroads
1920 L Street, N.W.
Washington, DC 20036

American Trucking Association
1616 P Street, N.W.
Washington, DC 20035

American Society of Traffic and
 Transportation, Inc.
547 West Jackson Boulevard
Chicago, IL 60606

Airline Pilots Association
1625 Massachusetts Avenue, N.W.
Washington, DC 20036

Air Line Employees Association
5600 S. Central Avenue
Chicago, IL 60638

Flight Engineers International Association
905 16th Street, N.W.
Washington, DC 20006

Air Transport Association of America
1000 Connecticut Avenue, N.W.
Washington, DC 20036

General Aviation Manufacturers Association
1025 Connecticut Avenue, Suite 1200-A
Washington, DC 20036

Government Jobs

Federal Job Information Center
U.S. Office of Personnel Management
1900 E Street, N.W., Room 1416
Washington, DC 20415

National Aeronautics and Space Administration
Washington, DC 20546

Office of Maritime Manpower,
Maritime Administration
U.S. Dept. of Commerce
Washington, DC 20235

United States Civil Service Commission
1900 E Street, N.W.
Washington, DC 20415

United States Department of Agriculture
Forest Service
Washington, DC 20250

The Armed Forces

Headquarters, U.S. Marine Corps
Washington, DC 20380

Department of the Navy
Office of Information
Washington, DC 20350

Department of Transportation
U.S. Coast Guard
Washington, DC 20593

Department of the Air Force
Headquarters Air Training Command
Randolph Air Force Base, TX 78150

Department of the Army
Office of the Secretary of the Army
Washington, DC 20310

Education and Training Information (Not Mentioned in Text)

Allied Health Education and Accreditation
535 N. Dearborn Street
Chicago, IL 60610

American Association for Community
and Junior Colleges
1 Dupont Circle, N.W., Suite 410
Washington, DC 20036

American Council on Education
1 Dupont Circle, N.W.
Washington, DC 20036

American Society for Training and
Development, Inc.
600 Maryland Avenue, S.W., Suite 305
Washington, DC 20024

Bureau of Apprenticeship and
Training
U.S. Department of Labor
601 D Street, N.W., Room 6100
Washington, DC 20213

Coalition of Adult Education Organizations
University of Connecticut
U-93
Storrs, CT 06268

Council for the Advancement of
Experimental Learning
10598 Marble Faun Court
Columbia, MD 21044

Directory of Postsecondary Schools with
  Occupational Programs, Public and Private, published
  by the National Center for Educational Statistics.
  Available from U.S. Government Printing Office,
  Washington, DC 20402

National Association for Industry Education
  Cooperation
235 Hendricks Boulevard
Buffalo, NY 14226

The American Vocational Association
2020 N. 14th Street
Arlington, VA 22201

United Business School Association
1730 M Street, N.W.
Washington, DC 20036

Index

A

Academy of Aeronautics, 215
Acly, Peter, 23
American Automobile Association, 38
American Bankers Association, 83–84, 207, 208
American Bar Association, 211
American Broadcasting Company, 32
American Council on Education, 11, 220
American Federation of Labor (AFL), 118
American Institute of Banking, 83
American Society for Personnel Administration, 8, 81, 146
Aoki, Rocky, 13
Apprenticeship Information Centers, 117
Apprenticeshop, 116
Aptitude tests, 47
Archer, Cynthia, 5
Arden, Elizabeth, 4
Armed Forces:
 Air Force information, 220
 apprenticeships in military, 100–101
 Army information, 220
 civilian occupations with military counterparts, 99
 Coast Guard information, 220
 decisions about joining, 103
 delayed entry program, 102
 enlistment policies, 103
 local recruiters, 102
 Marine Corps information, 219
 Navy information, 219
 training opportunities, 102–103
Art Instructions School, 123
Ash, Mary Kay, 5, 33
Associate and two-year degrees, 13, 82, 111
Association of Independent Colleges and Schools, 114
Attitude, importance of, 164
Austin, Sherri, 6, 136
Avery Fisher Hall, 70

B

Bartram, John, 120
Basic Student Charges, 2-Year Institutions, 124
Baxter, Neal, 98, 102
Belief in self, 179, 190, 191, 193, 194
Bergen Community College, 120
Bird, Caroline, 20
Bliss, Edwin, 169
Boehm, Martin, 93
Boles, Richard, 8
Brabec, Barbara, 34, 48, 139, 168, 180, 187, 191, 193
Braddock, Douglas, 11
Brekke, Nancy, 82
Brick Institute of America, 205
Broder, Shirley E., 83–84
Brown, Governor Jerry, 186
Brown, Helen Gurley, 4
Buechner, Matthew, 122
Bureau of Apprenticeship and Training, 117, 220
Bureau of Labor Statistics, 10, 11, 13, 24, 25, 75, 126
Burell Advertising, Inc., 22

C

California Governor's Advisory Board, 186
California State University, 8
Career counseling, 47, 137
"Career Strategies," 171
Carr, Eleanor, 83
Catafamo, Joann, 114
Catholic University of America, 76
Census Bureau, 25
Certified Professional Secretary Examination, 76
Chambers of Commerce, 137
Chastain, Sherry, 172
Cleary, Duncan, 70, 184, 190, 191
Coalition of Adult Education Organizations, 220
Coleman, John R., 24, 39
College Board Study, 12

Index

College Costs, 11–12
College Graduates:
   current job projections, 9–11
   degree no guarantee, 24, 25
   statistics, 10–11
   supply exceeding demand, 9, 12
   unemployment and underemployment, 9–11
Colorado State University, 193
Columbia School of Broadcasting, 123
Columbia University, 126
Computer training, necessity for, 76
Conference Board, Inc., the, 126
Congressional Gold Medal, 130
Congress of Industrial Organizations (CIO), 118
Consumer Information Center, 125
Consuming Passions, 179–180
Cooperative Education. *see* Work-study programs:
   Cooperative Office Education Programs, 18, 187
Cosmetology Accrediting Commission, 114
Cossman, E. J., 20
Council for Career Planning, Inc., 85
Council on Hotel, Restaurant, and Institutional Education, 217
Council on Social Work Education, 210
Coyne, John, 7, 115
Creative Cash, 34, 48, 191
Cremin, Lawrence A., 126
Crystal, John C., 8, 41–42, 66, 98, 102, 133–135, 137, 139, 146, 156, 158, 164, 170, 173, 174, 191
Culinary Institute of America, 217
C. W. Post College, 21

D

Dale Carnegie seminars, 164
Dana, Matt, 20
Dartus, Sandra, 187–189
Data Processing Management Association, 210
David-Shubin, Sharon, 13
Davis, Christopher, 109
Daydreaming, 44–45

DeCamp, Don, 12
Deer, Jean, 14–15, 21, 47, 113
DeSio, Joseph, 46
Determination, 179
Dictionary of Occupational Titles, 95
Diller, Barry, 32
Dinnebeil, Gary, 178
Directory of Accredited Home Study Schools, 124
Direct Mail Marketing Association, the, 209
Direct Selling Education Foundation, 209
Disney, Walt, 5
Distributive Education. *see* Work-study programs:
   Distributive Education Clubs of America, 120
Division of Occupational Outlook, 10, 11
Dorman, Terry, 5
Drive, importance of, 15, 55, 182, 191
Dun and Bradstreet, Inc., 55

E

Earnings:
   apprenticeships, 117
   high school vs. college, 25
   in non-college degree jobs, 26–31
Edna McConnell Clark Foundation, 24
Educational Institute of the American Hotel and Motel Association, 217
Education Council of the Graphic Arts, Inc., 206
18 Almanac, 167
Electronics Industries Association, 214
Electronics Technicians Association, 214
Employment agencies, 133, 134, 142, 143
Employment opportunities. *see also* Occupations:
   banking, 82–84
   business, 82–85
   clerical work, 74, 77
   communications, 71

computer-related jobs, 76–77
consulting, 93–95
creative and commercial art, 71
creative crafts, 71
franchising, 92–93
government, 85–87
health care, 87–89
mail order, 92
paraprofessionals, 72
performing arts, 70
retailing, 82
sales, 89–91
secretarial work, 75, 76, 77
service industries, 80–81
skilled trades and crafts, 67–69
small businesses vs. large corporations, 66, 136
technicians, 73
Encyclopedia of Careers and Vocational Guidance, 95
Encyclopedia of Associations, 95
Entrepreneurships, 53–58, 127
see also Self-employment
Entry-level jobs, starting with, 66, 76
Evaluating self:
autobiography writing, 41
journal keeping, 39
self-tests, 41, 43, 56, 57, 58
accomplishments and interests, identifying, 43–44, 146
Executive Female, The, 56
Executive recruiters, 133

F

Fadeff-Wood, Nikolette, 123
Failures, learning from, 183
Farm and Industrial Equipment Institute, 216
Fashion Institute of Design and Merchandising, the, 13, 82
Fashion Institute of Technology, 58, 190
Federal Job Information Center, 86, 219
Financial aid:
Bureau of Student Financial Assistance, 125
grants, 124

Guaranteed Student Loan Program, 125
loans, 124
National Direct Student Loan Program, 125
Need A Lift, 125
scholarships, 124
school financial aid offices, 124
Student Guide, 126
tuition payment plans, 124
United Student Aid Funds, 126
value of, 12
Vocational Loan Program, 126
Flexibility, 52, 185
Flight Engineers International Association, 219
Forging Industry Association, 204
Formby, Homer, 51–52, 182, 183, 184, 191, 192
Frome, Michael, 20, 38, 129, 130, 184, 193
Frost, Robert, 21

G

Gemological Institute of America, 123, 206
General Aviation Manufacturers Association, 219
General Education Development Certificates (GED), 117
General Foods International, 23
Getting Organized, 169
Getting Skilled, 7, 115
Getting Things Done, 169
Gift and Art Center, The, 92
Go Hire Yourself An Employer, 8, 34
"Good Morning America," 5
Government Printing Office, 95, 124
Group Attitude Corporation surveys, 12, 111
Grow Rich!—With Peace of Mind, 180
Gulfstream Aerospace Corporation, 34, 112, 113
Gunther, Max, 139

H

Handbook of Trade and Technical Careers and Training, 114

Index

Hannan, Diane, 71, 164
Hardigree, Ernest, 123
Hartman, David, 5
Hebert, Tom, 7, 115
Hecker, Daniel, 11
Help-wanted advertisements, 133, 136, 140, 141, 142
Hidden job possibilities, 138
High school graduates, opportunities for, 35
Hill Management Corporation, 110
Hill, Napoleon, 180
Hill, Suzanne, 110, 185, 190
Holland, John L., 44
Homemade Money, 34
Honorary degrees, 129
House of Bread, 52
Hudson, Gladys W., 56

Interviews:
    answering questions, 157
    asking questions, 157
    counteracting "No experience," 153
    discussing salary, 158
    emphasizing experience in place of college degree, 158
    handling not finishing college, 147, 159
    "information interviews," 136, 139
    learning job requirements, 157
    relating experience to job, 157
    showing enthusiasm, 159
Intrapreneurships, 23, 189
Investigate Before Investing, 93
Irish, Richard K., 7–8, 34, 144, 151, 152

I

Ideas, creating, 169, 179
Industrial Designers Society of America, 206
Instant Millionaires, 20
Institute for Research on Educational Finance and Governance, 9
Institute for the Certification of Engineering Technicians, 216
Institute of Life Insurance, 207
International Association of Firefighters, 203
International Association of Machinists and Aerospace Workers, 204
International Association of Wall and Ceiling Contractors, 203
International Council for Lathing & Plastering, 203
International Federation of Professional and Technical Engineers, 215
International Franchise Association, 92–93
International Society of Certified Electronics Technicians, 214
Internships:
    Kendell, Jane, 121
    National Society of Internships and Experiential Education, 121
    1985 INTERNSHIPS, 121

J

Jackson Brewery, 187, 188
Jackson, Tom, 159
Jakobson, Cathryn, 90
James, P. D., 4
Job banks, 133, 143
Job changing, 173
Job negotiations, 172, 173
Job proposals, 134, 135
Job Service, 143
Journal of Higher Education, 9

K

Kennedy, Marilyn Moats, 171
Kern, Gerald, 128, 153, 192
Kingery, Dr. Lionel Bruce, 118–119
Klein, Calvin, 190
Kostecka, Andrew, 93
Kuder Occupational Interest Survey, 47

L

L'Amour, Louis, 130
Labor Department, 13, 74, 75, 103, 117, 133, 143, 220
Lacey, Dr. William E., 164
Lady Finelle Cosmetics, 64
Lake Placid Resort Hotel, 171

LaLanne, Jack, 5
LaRouche, Janice, 132, 133, 146, 156, 160, 170, 173
Lauren, Ralph, 4
Leaders magazine, 184
Learning from people, 22, 95, 130
Leavitt, Arthur, 64
Leavitt, Crystal, 64
Leech, Richard, 70–71
Lee, Lance, 116
Leipzig, Arthur, 21, 182
Letters:
  cover, 153
  direct mail campaign, 139
  mailing lists, 138
  in answer to help-wanted ads, 141–142
  résumé-substitutes, 155–156
  to explore employment possibilities, 138
Levine, Michael, 121, 185, 186, 189
Lifelong Learning, 130, 165, 180
Lincoln Center, 70
Listening, 167, 168
Loebel, Terry, 19, 20
Long-range objectives, establishing, 136, 164
Lovejoy's Career and Vocational School Guide, 113
Love of work, 185, 190
Lusterman, Seymour, 126

M

MacFadyen, Tevere, 116
Mainliner magazine, 24, 39
Mainor, Gary A., 23, 152, 158
Making Vocational Choices: A Theory of Careers, 44
Management courses, 168, 169
Manufacturers' Agents National Association, 207
Margaritis, Charlene, 49, 122, 139, 159, 160
Marriott Hotels, 120
Martin, Michael Grant, 111
Martin, Steve, 5
Master Photo Dealers and Finishers Association, 204
McKuen, Rod, 4

Mechanical Contractors Association of America, 205
Meditech Pharmaceuticals, 128
Mefford, Mike, 116
Meister, Joseph, 52–53, 180, 183, 184, 191
Mentors, 166
Merrill, Robert, 5
Mier, David, 127, 128, 181, 182, 183
Mitzner, Fay, 58–59, 185
Morgan, Dr. James, 44–45
Morgan, Sharon, 22, 166, 189
Muir, John, 20
Murray, G. Dale, 6
Murray Industries, 6
Myths about college, 7

N

National Aeronautics and Space Administration, 219
National Alliance of Homebased Businesswomen, 207
National Alliance of TV and Electronic Service Association, 216
National Art Education Association, 207
National Association for Female Executives, 56
National Association for Licensed Practical Nurses, 211
National Association for Music Therapy, Inc., 213
National Association of Accountants, 207
National Association of Auto Trim Shops, 203
National Association of Barber Schools, Inc., 208
National Association of Broadcasters, 206
National Association of Dental Laboratories, 214
National Association of Insurance Women, 207
National Association of Legal Assistants, Inc., 211
National Association of Legal Secretaries, the, 209

Index

National Association of Metal Finishers, 203
National Association of Plumbing and Heating Contractors, 203
National Association of Realtors, 209
National Association of Schools of Music, 206
National Association of Securities Dealers, 90
National Association of Social Workers, 210
National Association of Trade and Technical Schools, 114, 115
National Association of Underwriters, 207
National Association of Wholesaler-Distributors, 208
National Automatic Sprinkler and Fire Control Association, 215
National Automobile Dealers, 208
National Barber Styling Career Center, 208
National Beauty Career Center, 217
National Cartoonists Society, 206
National Center for Education Statistics surveys, 11, 124
National Commission on Certification of Physician's Assistants, Inc., 210
National Committee on Household Employment, 218
National Council for Homemaker-Home Health Aide Services, 217
National Electrical Contractors Association, 203, 215
National Electric Sign Association, 216
National Federation of Paralegal Associations, Inc., 211
National Foundation of Funeral Services, 218
National Funeral Directors Association, 218
National Health Council, Inc., 212
National Home Business Report Newsletter, 34
National Home Study Council, 114, 123
National Industrial Recreation Association, 218
National Institute for Occupational Safety and Health, 213
National Institute for the Foodservice Industry, 80, 217
National League for Nursing, 212
National Machine Tool Builders Association, 205
National Mail Order Association, 209
National Organization for Women (NOW), 132
National Registry of Emergency Medical Technicians, 213
National Retail Merchants Association, the, 209
National Roofing Contractors Association, 202
National Shorthand Reporters Association, 209
National Society for Histotechnology, 213
National Society of Interior Designers, Inc., 207
National Task Force on the Image of the Secretary, the, 209
National Terrazzo and Mosaic Association, Inc., 204
National Therapeutical Recreation Society, 212
National Tooling and Machining Association, 203
Nepkie, Edward, 55
Newspaper Comics Council, Inc., the, 206
Networking, 139, 166
New York City Opera, 70
New York Community College, 13
New York magazine, 32
New York Times, The, 10, 13, 121, 133
Nicolato, Joseph, 34, 108–109, 159, 164, 182, 186, 187
Not having a degree:
 negative attitude, 189
 overcoming resistance from employers, 108, 158, 173
 threatened feeling, 190

O

Occupational Outlook Handbook, 95, 117

Index

Occupational Outlook Quarterly, 25, 98, 122
Occupational Projections and Training Data, 95
Occupations. see also Employment opportunities:
  goods-producing industries, 50–51
  not requiring college degree, 26–31
  service-producing industries, 50–51
  twenty fastest growing, 14
  with largest job growth, 65
Office Politics, 171
Olsten Corporation, the, 49, 74
On Your Own magazine, 116
Organizing self, 169
Originals by Fay, Ltd., 56

P

Painting and Decorating Contractors Association of America, 203
Parade magazine, 190
Paramount Pictures, 32
Paulson, Allen E., 34, 112, 184
"Peanuts," 123
People skills, 167
Personal development, 130, 165
Personnel departments, 133, 134, 136, 140, 174
Peterson, Roger Tory, 129
Phillips, A. J., 68
Piano Technicians Guild, Inc., 203
Pilenzo, Ronald C., 8, 24, 81, 146, 147, 153, 157, 173
Pilot Books, 43
Placement offices, 142
Plumbing-Heating-Cooling Information Center, 204
Poor's Register of Corporations, 137
Pope, Mary Ann, 74–75, 172, 181, 185, 192
Post-high school training:
  adult schools and evening courses, 109, 122
  apprenticeships, 12, 68, 87, 88, 103, 109, 116–118
  business and career schools, 12, 109, 113, 114
  community and junior colleges, 1, 109, 111
  company-sponsored training programs, 12, 109
  continuing education programs, 109, 122
  correspondence schools, 109, 122–124
  internships, 109, 121
  on-the-job learning and experience, 109, 128
  public library "universities," 109
  self-education, 109, 129
  seminars, 22, 95
  vocational/technical schools, 12, 109
  workshops, 22, 95–96
Power structures, identifying, 170–172
Presidential Medal of Freedom, 129
Professional journals, 141
Professional Photographers of America, Inc., 206
Professional Secretaries International, 76, 209
Professional Consultant, The, 94
Promotions, 172
Prudential Life Insurance Company, 111
Public Relations Society of America, Inc., 206

R

Raises, 172
Reading, importance of, 130, 180, 181
Reading list, 196–202
Refrigeration Service Engineers Society, 216
Relocating, 175
Responsibility, asking for, 168
Résumés:
  as predictive tools, 134
  chronological, 148, 149
  functional, 147, 149, 150, 151, 152
  planning, 146, 147
  résumé-substitute letters, 156
  "talking résumés," 146
  writing, 147
Rickenbacker, Eddie, 5
Risk-taking, 183, 184

Index

Roberts, Stephen F., 76
Rockefeller Center, 46
Rogak, Lisa, 178–180, 189
Rumberger, Russell W., 9, 10, 76

S

Sacrifices, 183, 184
Sales and Marketing Executives – International, 208
Sargent, Jon, 10, 11, 24
Schlenger, Sunny, 169
Schmidt, Michele Hogan, 18–19, 122
Schultz, Charles, 123
Security Industry Association, 208
Self-employment, 14
  see also Entrepreneurships
Sheet-Metal and Air Conditioning Contractors' National Association, Inc., 204
Sheet Metal Workers International Association, 204
Shenson, Howard L., 8, 55, 93–94, 183
Sheraton Hotels, 18, 19, 122
Shields, Dorothy, 119
Skovholt, Dr. Thomas, 44–45
Slonaker, Harry, 167
Small Business Administration, 55
Snelling and Snelling, 13
Social amenities, 165, 166
Society for Technical Communications, Inc., 216
Society of American Florists, the, 208
Society of American Florist and Ornamental Horticulturists, 205
Society of American Foresters, 210
Society of Automotive Engineers, Inc., the, 216
Speaking up, 181
Specialized training and skills, need for, 66, 109
Standard Rate and Data Directory of Business Magazines, 141
Stanford University, 9
Stanley Home Products, 33
State Apprenticeship Councils, 117
State Boards for Dispensing Opticians, 88
State Civil Service Commissions, 86
State Departments of Education, 114
State Employment Services, 47, 86, 95, 117, 137, 143
Steil, Dr. Lyman K., 167
Strategies for Women at Work, 132, 170
Strong-Campbell Interest Inventory, 47
Success, definition of, 192

T

Taylor, Emilie, 80
Temporary service jobs, 49, 74, 143, 144
The Address Book: How To Reach Anyone Who's Anyone, 186
The Case Against College, 20
The Complete Guide To Writing Nonfiction, 20
The Luck Factor, 139
Think and Grow Rich, 180
This Way Out: A Guide to Alternatives to Higher Education, 7
Thomas, Richard, 5
Thomson McKinnon Securities, 90
Tile Contractors Association of America, Inc., 205
Time management, 169
Trade publications, 141
Traits to develop, 34, 182, 183, 184, 185, 186, 190, 191
Twain, Mark, 20
Trans World Airlines, 112
Truman, Harry, 5
20th Century-Fox Film Corporation, 32
28 Days To A Better Job, 158

U

Unions, role of, 118–119
United Automobile, Aerospace & Agricultural Implement Workers, 118
United Brotherhood of Carpenters and Joiners, 118
United Business School Association, 221
United States Civil Service Commission, 219

University of Idaho, 38
University of Rochester, 70
University of Southern California, 8
University of Wisconsin, 20
United States Department of Education, 114, 127
United States International University, 54, 164
United States Office of Personnel examinations, 86

V

Val-Pak, 19
Vernon, Lillian, 92
Ver Standig, Helen. see Madame Wellington
Visibility, 189
Vocational interests tests, 47
VOC-ED Journal, 109
Volunteer work, 49, 147
Volvo of America Corporation, 34, 108

W

Ward, Peter, 25
Washington Post, 38

Water Pollution Control Federation, 216
WCB Group Publishers, 23, 152, 158
Wellington, Madame, 54, 185
Wharton School, 54
Where Do I Go from Here with My Life?, 8
Wider Opportunities for Women, 41
Wilkinson, Bud, 186
Wilkins, Tobe, 130
Winning the Salary Game, 172
Winston, Stephanie, 169
Woman's Day magazine, 151
Working "smart," 171
"Workshops for Women," 133
Work-study programs, 109, 119–121, 124, 125

Y

Yellow Pages, 137
You Don't Have to Be a Genius to Land a Computer Job, 76

Z

Zaborer, Ed, 5